Christmas
Through a Child's Eyes

*True Stories That Capture
the Wonder of the Season*

EDITED BY
HELEN SZYMANSKI

adamsmedia
Avon, Massachusetts

Published by Adams Media,
an F+W Publications Company
57 Littlefield Street
Avon, MA 02322
www.adamsmedia.com

ISBN 10: 1-59869-644-0
ISBN 13: 978-1-59869-644-8

Printed in the United States of America.

J I H G F E D C B A

Library of Congress Cataloging-in-Publication Data
is available from the publisher.

This publication is designed to provide accurate and authoritative information with regard to the subject matter covered. It is sold with the
understanding that the publisher is not engaged in rendering legal,
accounting, or other professional advice. If legal advice or other expert
assistance is required, the services of a competent professional person
should be sought.
—From a *Declaration of Principles* jointly adopted by a Committee of the
American Bar Association and a Committee of Publishers and Associations

Many of the designations used by manufacturers and sellers to distin-
guish their products are claimed as trademarks. Where those designations appear in this book and Adams Media was aware of a trademark
claim, the designations have been printed with initial capital letters.

This book is available at quantity discounts for bulk purchases.
For information, please call 1-800-289-0963.

*This book is dedicated to the memory of Barbara Anton.
She had a way with words and a lot of great stories to tell.*

Contents

Acknowledgments

A special thank you is extended to all who helped take this book from idea to reality: my family, my agent, Kate Epstein, all of the authors who submitted their work—and especially all of our readers—my in-house editor, Andrea Norville, and everyone at F+W Publications, Inc. I'd also like to offer my sincerest gratitude to Paul Harvey—the Voice of America—for his glowing endorsement, and also to June Westgaard, his loyal assistant, for being such a lovely person. Thank you for believing in me and for being there when I needed you. In closing, I extend my deepest gratitude to the Lord, who gives me great visions, holds my hand when I need it, and always, always believes in me.

Introduction

L ike you, I love Christmas. And how could we not? Everything from decorations to Baby Jesus work overtime to keep a smile on our faces. Every year—without fail—holiday magic is so thick I can serve it to my family on a spoon. Gift giving and receiving seems to have the same effect on each of us as it did on the Grinch—you can actually feel your heart swell!

Christmastime is magical. Nothing else touches us quite the same. Christmas and the memories it stirs up are thought provoking as well as humbling. It's a time when the best of our character spills forth and the worse part of our personality disappears. We are kinder, more understanding, more apt to forgive. If it were Christmas everyday, perhaps hatred would be wiped out, wars would no longer need to be fought, and neighbors and families would remember to love one another.

Because I truly believe in the miracle of Christmas, it is my hope that through *Christmas Through a Child's Eyes: True Stories That Capture the Wonder of the Season* we can keep those special, magical feelings alive year round. As you read the memories my authors have graciously chosen to share, I ask that you also recall your own favorite memories and share them with a loved one or neighbor—better yet, share them with a stranger—so that the wonderful feeling of Christmas can continue to flow unhindered from one heart to the next.

I hope, like me, you'll keep this book nearby to warm your heart and renew your spirit and remind you of the things in life that really matter. From my heart to yours—wishing you a Merry Christmas every single day of the year.

—*Helen Szymanski*

Shared Popcorn

BY J. HOGAN CLARK

The winter of 1948 was bitter cold. December popped up on the calendar with blustery winds and torrents of snow and freezing rain. But my sister, Carol, and I hardly noticed. December also meant Christmas, and we couldn't wait for the festivities to begin.

One evening, as Christmas Eve neared, Mom and Dad decided to treat Carol and me to a movie. We almost never got to go to a movie and we were ecstatic. For a grand total of sixty cents (the movie admission was fifteen cents, popcorn was a nickel, and soft drinks were a dime), my sister and I could have an entire evening of entertainment and snacks. It just didn't get any better than that.

Though it had stopped snowing, a fierce north wind cut through my heavy coat as I climbed into the backseat of our old Oldsmobile. On the trip to the movie house, I rubbed my hands together to stay warm and to keep my excitement from bubbling over. Carol stared straight ahead, her right hand clasped into a fist, a death grip on our money as the car bounced and slid down the road. The roads were still treacherous, with thick pockets of accumulated snow and ice covering most of the surfaces, but Dad had maneuvered these roads before in inclement weather. He skillfully coasted to a stop in front of the movie house with plenty of time to spare. Carol and I exchanged grins. We wouldn't miss the cartoons, a possibility we'd both worried over.

As soon as we exited the vehicle, Dad waved goodbye and drove off, leaving us to our own adventures. The wind whipped wisps of snow across streets and down the sidewalks in a mini blizzard, and the whistling sound it made as it rushed around buildings and through tree branches seemed to intensify the cold. I couldn't wait to get inside the movie house!

As we stood in line shivering, I noticed a young girl about my sister's age, and a smaller sibling, probably her brother, who looked to be about five years old. Their shoulders hunched against the frigid wind, they huddled together next to the movie house entryway. Though the girl's chin was tucked beneath a heavy scarf and the boy wore galoshes and thick mittens, the stabbing wind tugged at their lightweight jackets and I knew they had to be freezing. To make matters worse, the little boy was sobbing, his tears leaving shiny wet tracks down his red, swollen face.

As I watched, the girl's bare hands dove in and out of the pockets in her pink jacket and blue jeans. As soon as her cold hands would find a pocket, she'd manipulate the contents, searching in vain for something. Visibly upset, she attempted to comfort her brother. Try as she might, however, the girl couldn't bring closure to her brother's tears, nor find what she so desperately searched for.

Though I knew it was rude to stare, I couldn't tear my eyes away from the scene unfolding before me. As the ticket line dwindled, my sister and I drew closer to the distraught youngsters. That's when I heard the young girl explain to her brother that she couldn't find the last twenty-five cents.

Evidently, they, too, had been dropped off at the movie house, and wouldn't be picked up until after the movie. And without the missing twenty-five cents, they could no longer purchase their movie tickets.

I felt a pang of sympathy; I could imagine that happening to my sister and me instead of them. Not knowing what else to do, I turned my eyes away sadly and stared at the back of my sister's jacket.

It seemed like an eternity before we reached the ticket booth window. With tickets in hand, Carol turned and began walking toward the entry doors. By now, the boy's wails had subsided somewhat, but his little body shook uncontrollably as his sister wrapped her arms about him in an attempt to soothe away the hurt and cold.

Obediently, I followed my sister, fully expecting her to open the door and walk in. Abruptly, she stopped. As I maneuvered past her to prevent myself from knocking her over, she turned and handed two dimes and a nickel to the girl with the sobbing brother. It was as if the Christmas Spirit had descended on her that evening, because out of nowhere, her compassion for the two stranded, freezing children overcame her desire for popcorn and a soft drink.

I understood what she felt, because I felt it, too. The look of surprise and pure elation on the other children's faces made me feel ten feet tall! I was sure my chest would swell to the point of popping the buttons off my coat! A heated flush raced through me and I smiled as wide as a Jack-o-lantern. I was so proud of my sister that I no longer felt the cold. I basked in the warmth of her goodness that night, and am happy to say that over the years the feeling of pride for what she had done has never gone away. I don't recall what movie we saw that night, but I will never forget the bag of popcorn we shared. It was the best bag of popcorn I've ever consumed, and all because I shared it with the best sister anyone could ask for.

The School Desks

BY CONNIE STURM CAMERON

As I trudged through the softly falling snow, Christmas lights gradually illuminated the homes in my neighborhood. It was Christmas Eve, 1967, and I was almost done with my paper route. The hushed beauty of the winter dusk scene invited me to slow my anxious steps. My ten-year-old mind, awed by the beauty of nature, wondered why the world seemed so quiet when it snowed. Even the sound of my own breath seemed to reverberate in my ears.

Normally, I kept my newspapers in the basket on my bike and rode up and down the driveways in my neighborhood to deliver them, but when it snowed, it seemed easier to don my rubber boots and walk to each front porch. My favorite house on Connway Drive was where my best friend, Cindy, lived. We had promised to call each other as soon as we finished opening our gifts the next day—as long as the party line wasn't in use.

Lights were being turned on in houses up and down the street and when I walked to their front doors to drop the newspaper, I heard more and more laughter and excitement: Families were gathering in anticipation of Christmas festivities.

After tossing my final newspaper, I began my trek home. It was time for dinner, and as usual, I was starving. But it was hard to hurry. There is something magical about Christmas Eve, and that night I felt it in the air. It was as if every child in the whole world was holding their breath, wondering if their long-awaited GI Joe or Thumbelina doll would be under the tree when they awoke the next morning.

When I finally arrived home, I stopped in front of our house and stared—it was so beautiful. The colored lights lit up the night sky and the snow surrounding the lights seemed to absorb the color of each bulb. My father and older brother, Tim, had strung large, red Christmas bulbs all along the roof of our ranch home, and had trimmed the two blue spruce trees flanking our driveway with hundreds of vibrant blue lights. At that moment, as my eyes darted back and forth between the two decorations, I couldn't decide if red or blue was my favorite. Dad had even decorated the bushes bordering the front of our house with multicolored lights, and Mom had hung red flickering Christmas bells in our bedroom windows.

My heart sang with the beauty of it all.

Oh blessed Christmas! One more day to go! *What would the next twenty-four hours hold for me?* I tried hard to remember all the things I had wanted for gifts. My sister was too old for her Barbie dolls, so I had a lot of her hand-me-downs; however, it would be nice to get the new Skipper doll. My real love, though, was playing schoolteacher. I even had a makeshift school set up in our basement. My younger brothers, Danny and Gary, were my students, along with Cindy. I had saved my paper-route money and bought a chalkboard, chalk, and other small school supplies. My "students" used an old lawn chair and overturned buckets for seats, and a well-worn card table as their desk.

I spent hours planning lessons and giving tests. But if it weren't for the treats my mother graciously allowed us to have each day, I'm certain my students would not have participated. The promise of homemade potato candy with peanut butter swirled inside or no-bake oatmeal cookies kept everyone pretending to be interested for hours!

I hoped to have a real classroom one day, and secretly prayed God would work it out.

"Are you sure all you want for Christmas is a Skipper doll?" my mother had asked just the other day.

"Yeah. Well, maybe some more school supplies . . . like scissors and colored pencils," I added.

Before going to bed that night, my sister and I grabbed one flashlight and my three brothers grabbed the other. That way, if we woke up in the middle of the night, we could sneak into the living room to see how many presents Santa and our parents had left for us. Because our father was a pressman for the local newspaper and brought home the butt-ends from the huge rolls of newsprint paper that was used on the printing presses, presents for all seven in our family would be wrapped alike. Our living room would be a sea of off-white boxes in every size and shape.

Finally, Christmas morning arrived. I was certain our squeals of laughter and cries of joy could be heard throughout our neighborhood with each gift that was opened, especially when Gary got his new bicycle! My older siblings and I were all jealous because we had to share the same beat-up bike. Our tradition, though, was that each year one of us kids would get something big. This year it was Gary's turn.

And yes, a Skipper doll was under the tree for me, along with a new Trouble game and some more supplies for my makeshift school. I jumped for joy at the new supplies. Word had gotten out about the fun—snacks—we were having, and more neighbor kids expressed an interest in coming over during the Christmas break.

As the last gift was unwrapped and each of us gathered our treasured piles to take to our rooms, Mom said, "Lets all head downstairs. Santa has left one last gift there."

We dashed down the steps two at a time. There was a sheet covering something large in the middle of the basement floor . . . in the middle of my schoolroom.

"Connie," Dad said. "You get to take the sheet off."

Me? Really?

I had no idea what could be so big—bigger than a bike!

"Hurry up!" my siblings squealed, thrilled there was one last large gift and hoping I'd share whatever it was. As I ripped the sheet off, it uncovered not one, not two, but three old-fashioned school desks! They each had a seat attached on the front. They were perfect!

"They're not perfect; they're old and kind of beat-up," Mom said, the corners of her mouth lifting into a knowing smile, "but we thought you could get some use out of them."

Finally, I could have a real school! I couldn't wait to call Cindy and tell her the good news!

That was forty years ago, and I still have one of those desks. My mother and sister opted to keep the other two. The date "1913" is branded into one of the wrought-iron legs, and the hand-carved initials of childhood loves are still embedded in the wood. Recently, my husband suggested we sand the desktop down and stain it to make it look as good as new, but I declined the offer. God—who alone shared my dream—knows my desk will always look perfect to me.

The Sweetness of Giving

by Megan (Molly) D. Willome

A s a child, I loved candy, but the only time I got any was on a holiday. And at my house, the only candy we ever had was homemade fudge. My family wasn't poor, but my mother didn't believe in wasting money. While her motto was "Why buy it if you can make it," I secretly longed for store-bought, prepackaged treats.

As the Christmas holiday drew near, my first grade teacher, Mrs. Cunningham, made an announcement: it was time to start thinking about the annual Christmas party. She concluded by saying that each child was to bring a small gift to exchange. My eyes widened. The Christmas party would be another chance to get genuine, grade-A candy! When Mom picked me up that day, I told her about the party. "Mrs. Cunningham said to bring something that doesn't cost too much," I added.

Mom smiled at me in the rearview mirror. "I have the perfect craft! We can make light switch covers. It's inexpensive, and will be a gift that no one else has."

My heart fell. "Can't we just buy something?" I asked.

"Of course not," Mom answered. "This will be more fun!"

That afternoon, Mom made a sample light switch cover using red felt for a frame, green felt for a tree, and sequins for ornaments. I tried to follow her example, but the finished product looked like a preschooler had made it.

On the day of the party, I watched each child place their gift on Mrs. Cunningham's desk. I held tightly to my home-made gift, hoping none of my friends would end up with it. As I watched, one boy slapped his present onto the teacher's desk and my heart leapt with joy—it was a LifeSavers Sweet Storybook! It was only decorated with a big bow, but that was the gift I wanted! It held eight rolls of LifeSavers, two each of Butter Rum, Pep O Mint, Crysto Mint, and Wild Cherry. My mouth watered as I joined the other children sitting in a circle on the reading rug.

"Don't open these yet," said Mrs. Cunningham as she passed one gift to each student. Every child in the room stared at a girl named Dana when Mrs. Cunningham passed the Life-Savers Sweet Storybook to her.

Once the gifts were distributed, Mrs. Cunningham explained that as she read *The Night Before Christmas,* each time she turned a page, we were to pass the gift we held in our lap to the next person. Whichever gift was in your hand when she ended the book became yours.

I watched the candy move around the room, anxious for it to be in my lap. When I finally held it, I waited my turn to pass it on. But just then, Mrs. Cunningham read the final line in the book.

"And to all a good night," she said with a flourish and closed the book. I stared at the candy in my lap. I could hardly believe my luck!

Fully aware that some children had received candy and others had received homemade gifts, our teacher instructed us to leave our gifts in the classroom before going outside for a long recess.

I placed the candy on my desk and ran out the door. On the swings, I pumped my legs until I was going as high as I could. As I sailed back and forth, I thought about the LifeSavers Sweet Storybook. *Which flavor should I try first? Should I eat them all at once or should I eat one a day and make them last?*

After a few minutes, Mrs. Cunningham opened the classroom door and motioned to me. "Molly, would you mind coming in? I'd like to talk to you."

The teacher had never summoned me before, and my initial thought was tragic: *Is she going to take away my candy?*

Instead, Mrs. Cunningham smiled and patted me on the head. "You made a beautiful gift, Molly. Do you know who received it?"

"No," I answered as politely as I could.

"Dana did," said Mrs. Cunningham. She bent down so we were eye level. "Are you two friends?"

I looked at the candy on my desk and shook my head. "She sits on the other side of the room."

Mrs. Cunningham smiled. "She thinks your gift is very pretty. But, you see, Dana's home has no light switches." I turned to the teacher and scrunched up my face, trying to understand what that meant. Mrs. Cunningham smiled. "Dana's house is so old that it isn't wired for electricity, and electricity is expensive. Dana offered your gift to me. Would you like to have it back?"

"You can keep it," I whispered.

Mrs. Cunningham smiled. "Thank you. I'll find something else in my desk for Dana. I usually have a few little things hidden away." Mrs. Cunningham turned to her desk and began to search.

I glanced out the window and spotted Dana playing by herself in one corner of the playground. *How could a house not have electricity? How did the family turn on the lights?* Then I had an awful thought. I glanced at the candy on my desk again. *If they didn't have electricity, could they afford to have candy in their stockings?*

Without a second thought, I turned to Mrs. Cunningham.

"Dana can have my gift," I said quickly.

My teacher looked up in surprise. "Are you sure?"

I nodded.

"Thank you," she said, a smile lighting up her face. "You don't know how much this will mean to her."

When Mom arrived that afternoon to pick me up from school, Mrs. Cunningham took her aside. I watched nervously as they talked. After a few minutes, Mrs. Cunningham summoned me to join them. I walked slowly to the teacher's desk for the second time that day. When I got to the front of the classroom, Mrs. Cunningham opened the big drawer in her desk and handed me a Christmas tree ornament.

I stared at it in wonder.

"I'm sorry it isn't wrapped," she said as I continued to stare.

In my whole life, I had never received a store-bought ornament. Mom and I made all the Christmas decorations for our tree from scratch. Finally, with eyes glistening, I opened the box and pulled out a wooden girl on a swing.

I felt Mom's arm slide around my shoulders. "She looks just like you!" she said. I nodded, hugging my mother's legs happily.

The next morning, when I reached out to turn on the light in my bedroom, my fingers found the sample light switch cover Mom had made. I ran my fingers over the sequins. They were the same shape as LifeSavers. For a moment, I could almost taste the flavors: Butter Rum, Pep O Mint, Crysto Mint, and Wild Cherry. Then I thought of Dana tasting each flavor, perhaps for the first time, and I smiled.

I could wait until Christmas for candy—even if it was homemade!

Santa's Messenger

BY LYNN RUTH MILLER

I was born at the end of the Depression, in a time when we treated strangers differently than we do today. In those days, people often knocked at our back door to ask for food and my mother always invited them inside for a hot bowl of soup or a sandwich. It was not that we were wealthy—no one had extra money in the early '30s—but we were quick to share what we had because we knew that one upset to our own budget and we, too, would not have enough to eat or a warm place to sleep.

One man appeared at our door several times a week. He was very different from most of the vagrants that sat at my mother's table. He refused to take anything for nothing. "Let me sweep the walk for you, Missus," he'd say, or, "Why don't you let me hang out those sheets for you today?"

He was unshaven and wore drab, patched clothes, obviously salvaged from the dustbin. He used to keep a potato in his mouth, and when he smiled, you could see it through the spaces between his tobacco-stained teeth. He rolled the potato around in his mouth and tucked it behind his molars when he spoke. That was why everyone called him Potato Tom.

Potato Tom seemed to enjoy the tasks my mother gave him and did them with great energy. As winter approached, his clothes got shabbier and he wore no gloves or scarf as protection from the relentless Ohio cold. His hands were spotted with reddened chilblains and as soon as he stood still, he shivered uncontrollably.

"Would you like to borrow a coat, Tom?" Mama would ask. "You must be freezing. I have an old scarf we never wear. Let me give it to you."

He always smiled and shook his head. "I'm used to being outdoors, Missus," he'd say. "But a hot bowl of something would sure feel good right about now."

Of all the people who came to our door, Tom was my favorite. I sat across from him at the table while he ate and listened to stories about places he'd been. "I remember one winter I spent in Floriday," he said, fanning himself as he did so. "It was so hot there you never wore a coat and you couldn't be hungry—what with oranges and coconuts free for the picking." He got a faraway look in his eye, as if remembering. Then he shook his head. "But then times got bad and I couldn't get work so I walked up north."

I looked at his torn shoes. The laces had disappeared long ago. He now secured his shoes to his feet with pieces of rope. "You walked all the way from Floriday?" I asked in awe. "Didn't your feet get tired?"

He shook his head. "In this life, honey, you do what you have to do. Ain't that right, Missus?" he asked my mother.

Mama's eyes looked very red and she sniffled like she had a cold. "I have some meatloaf from last night I could warm up for you, Tom," she said. "How does that sound?"

Tom was very polite when he ate, and even though I was only four years old, I knew his manners were a lot better than mine. He never dropped food all over his clothes the way I did and he never forgot to wipe his mouth with a napkin.

I took his hand when he stood to leave and squeezed it, "Come back, Tom, and tell me about Floriday."

He glanced over my head at my mother and then he nodded. "Maybe later in the week, honey," he said. "When your mama needs some windows washed."

I discovered a new truth about Santa Claus the year Tom came to our house. Even though we did not observe the religious ceremony of Christmas, I believed in the jolly benefactor with all my heart, and had long imaginary conversations with him weeks before the big day when my mother took me to LaSalle's to sit on Santa's lap. On that day, my mother dressed me in my very best snowsuit with little white flowers on the collar and a bonnet to match.

"Santa will just love you!" she said as we ran to catch the streetcar downtown.

As we walked through the slush and ice on the downtown streets, I noticed that every single corner had a Santa ringing his bell for people to contribute to the Salvation Army.

"Why are there so many Santas walking around the street?" I asked suspiciously. "I thought only one Santa came down the chimney on Christmas night."

"They're Santa's helpers, Lynnie Ruth," Mother explained. "He's very busy this time of year. He can't be everywhere in the world at once."

I frowned. "I thought he was magic."

"He is," she answered. "Just look how many people he has scattered across the globe telling boys and girls that their wishes will come true!"

"Does Santa tell all these helpers what to say?"

She nodded. "He sends them messages from his heart."

When we entered the department store, I held my mother's hand and tried to be very quiet while we waited in line. When at last it was my turn, I ran up the steps and jumped on the bearded man's lap. But when I looked into his eyes, I saw truth.

"You're not Santa!" I cried in surprise. "You're Potato Tom!"

From behind that beard came the voice I had heard so many times at my mother's kitchen table. "Today, I am your very own Santa Claus, Lynnie Ruth," he said. "Santa sent me down from the North Pole to tell you he knew what a very good girl you are and that he will bring you that Shirley Temple doll you want, and a little stove that really works."

Awestruck, I gazed up at him. "How did you know I wanted all that?"

Tom's eyes twinkled just like the picture books said they would and his pillow-stuffed belly shook with laughter. "Why, Santa told me!" he said.

Something about him looked different. I peered into his mouth and then realized why. "What happened to your potato?"

He smiled. "I got so excited when I saw you standing in line that I swallowed it!"

My mouth dropped open. "Then that's what I'll give *you* for Christmas! A brand new potato!" I said as I scrambled off his lap in order to give the next child a turn.

As we walked away, I turned to my mother. "How did Tom get to be Santa's helper? Did he walk to the North Pole like he did from Floriday?"

Mother shook her head. When she spoke, I could barely understand her words because she was afflicted with sudden congestion. "I guess he just looked up at the winter sky and asked God to help him help himself."

"You mean God told Santa Claus to hire Tom?" I asked.

My mother shook her head, "No, Lynn Ruth," she said. "God gave him nobility, and that's the most important qualification for the job."

The Adventures of Baby Jesus

BY CHERYL K. PIERSON

No one loved Baby Jesus like I did. He was my constant holiday companion. From the moment we took the nativity set from the box to decorate for Christmas, I carried Him with me.

I couldn't just let Him lay in the cardboard manger unattended. The nativity was old, even older than I was. It was made of thick brown cardboard, as was the manger. A few pieces of straw were glued into it, but not nearly enough to make a good baby bed!

I thought of Baby Jesus as the little brother I had begged for and never got. Someone had to take care of Him. Jesus, Mary, and Joseph, as well as two of the attending sheep, were made of plaster. They'd chip or break if not handled with great care.

At four years old, I knew how to be careful—especially with Baby Jesus and His entourage. The proof of what could happen was all too evident in poor Mary. Two years ago, someone had been too rough, and there had been a terrible accident. The blue shawl that covered Mary's back had been broken, revealing a ghastly silver rod that disappeared into what was left of her shawl, gathered about her feet. At the top, the exposed rod extended into the back of her head. Mary had to be positioned "just so," to keep the world from seeing that horrid sliver of metal that kept her in one piece.

I couldn't help wondering if my Baby Jesus had a rod running through Him like His mother did. I finally convinced myself He didn't—He was a lot smaller, and there probably weren't any rods that tiny. And, being the Son of God, He didn't need a rod.

Joseph struck a thoughtful pose, kneeling beside Mary, both of them watching the perpetually empty manger. He was a bit wobbly since someone, in a terrible accident, had chipped quite a chunk from his orange and yellow robe. Kneeling was a challenge for him now, but not impossible—especially if he leaned a little on Mary or the manger or one of the poor chalk sheep who had all lost their tails somewhere along the way.

The Three Kings added color to the scene in robes of red, green, and purple. They had been bought at a later date, and were made of a thick, brittle plastic rather than plaster. They carried gifts that were of no value to a baby.

Balthazar's arm was missing. At one time, he had been extending his gift of frankincense—perfume! I cut a small blanket of green velveteen from the back of a dress in my closet and laid it over his stump. Jesus would enjoy a warm blanket in that drafty stable more than an old bottle of perfume.

Melchior knelt in humble repose, a hinged gold box in his hands. As if Jesus could open a box! Being four, I didn't have any "baby toys" left to offer, but I did have something better than what those supposed "wise men" brought.

I had colored marbles—something pretty for Jesus to look at. And I had crayons to color Him a picture. I imagined Baby Jesus would be getting mighty tired of Christmas music right about then—it was all He ever heard. I headed for my collection of 45s and settled one onto the turntable of my record player. Johnny Horton belted out the strains of "North to Alaska" while Baby Jesus and I danced together.

We didn't have a Drummer Boy for our nativity set, and I felt the loss keenly. I wanted our Baby Jesus to have the best nativity in the world. It was bad enough that two years ago there had been a terrible accident and someone had irreparably broken the only shepherd we had. Now, we had sheep milling in the stable with no shepherd, and no Little Drummer Boy, either.

Luckily, this was a situation I could easily remedy. I had four different colors of Play-Doh. After a long, tedious ten minutes, I had what I considered to be a passable Drummer Boy and his drum—complete with tiny drumsticks.

The other Wise Man, Caspar, was in bad shape, but there was no help for it. Someone, in a terrible accident, had broken off his head. My mother had reglued it, but after it had dried, the glue line showed as if he had not washed his neck after a month of hot Oklahoma summer days. I tied my Annie Oakley bandana around him. It covered his broken neck, and gave him a mysterious look—like a western Superman carrying his leather-bound gift box. It contained myrrh, which I knew was a kind of oil. Finally, something Baby Jesus could use!

We had a cow, a donkey, and an angel made from the same hard plastic as the Wise Men. In a terrible accident two years ago, the donkey's rear had been broken off. I put him at the back of the stable. The cow was lying on the ground, its legs folded beneath it. It must have seen whatever had befallen the donkey and gotten to the ground in time to avoid disaster.

The angel baffled me, though. Evidently, she had not been so quick or lucky. There was the same brown glue line across her right wing that poor Caspar suffered at the neck, and I was fresh out of bandanas. I figured she had slipped off the stable roof a couple of years ago. She never watched where she was going, because she was looking up to the heavens, singing. Maybe, her being an angel and all, that injury would heal. By next Christmas, we might not even be able to see it.

I brought Baby Jesus out of my pocket and gave Him a kiss. It was then that I noticed what bad shape He was in. I had loved Him too much! His baby hair was spotty, as if the paint had been worn off in places. His body was dappled unevenly and His nose was almost completely flat.

But, His blue eyes were open, sparkling joyously. I knew He must have caught a glimpse of His nativity set. I held Him out to get a good look.

I had taped a freshly colored picture of a boy and his puppy inside the stable wall. It covered the window and kept out the night wind. I showed Him His bed with the marbles around the base of it, and the sheep on guard to keep them from rolling out of the stable.

Caspar's bandana looked mighty fine, safety-pinned across the glue line. I had done as much as I could for the others; hidden the donkey's broken rear and Mary's metal rod, and let Joseph surreptitiously lean against the kneeling cow so he wouldn't fall.

I laid Baby Jesus in His bed and covered Him with Balthazar's new offering—the blanket.

Just then, my mother rounded the corner, the green velveteen dress in her hands and a look of disbelief in her eyes. "Cheryl, do you know what happened to this dress?" she asked sternly. I swallowed hard and leaned against the nativity for support. I only hoped Baby Jesus could help me now.

Christmas Eve Delivery

BY CHRISTINE E. COLLIER

W e lived in a small, two-bedroom, bungalow-style house, situated in the country, atop a small hill. We were a small family—two parents and four children—but we were about to add a Collie puppy to our numbers. I knew this because Mom had shared the secret with me. The puppy was hiding in a dark basement not far from the coal bin. It was my job to make some sort of noise whenever the puppy yipped so that my brother, Mark, wouldn't hear. Mark, two years younger than me, loved to walk the hills looking for blackberries and hickory nuts, and a dog would be a welcome companion. He'd be so surprised on Christmas morning!

At the age of eleven, I was the eldest. My best friend lived next door, had an upright piano in her recreation room, and took piano lessons. Just the fact that she had a rec room, and they had board games like Life, Clue, and Monopoly sitting on top of their piano, was fascinating to me. Whenever she played *Moonlight Sonata,* I thought it was the most beautiful song I had ever heard. I dreamed of learning how to play the piano. My mother listened to my dream and soon, I realized, it had become her dream as well. We both know there was not really room in our small living room for a piano. We also knew piano practice would cause problems when the family watched television, but still my mother and I dreamed on.

Having a puppy in the basement was enough to keep Mom and me on our toes that evening. We fluttered from one room to the next, talking loudly and making unnecessary sounds to cover up the puppy noises that floated up through the floor vents. Mom was being very mysterious today, and in my heart of hearts, I felt something else—besides a secret puppy in the basement—was going on. She seemed awfully worried that the front steps were snowy and wondered if the roads were slippery now that it had begun to snow.

Though it was still early, Mom insisted we go to bed soon and remain in our bedrooms even if we heard something. It was too early for Santa to show up—Daddy wasn't even home yet! I couldn't help but wonder what she thought we might hear.

By the time eight o'clock rolled around, we had no choice. Wearing our new Christmas Eve pajamas, we trudged off to bed. It was much too early, and though we tried to sleep, we were not the least bit tired.

I heard Mom's footsteps as she moved from one room to the next, and watched as the outside lights were turned on and off many times. I lay in my bed awake, remembering to cough or talk loudly to my brothers in their bunk bed every time I heard a noise from the basement. Then I heard something else! *Was that the sound of a piano key being struck?* My heart leapt for joy, although I said nothing to my brothers. I was so anxious and excited I was awake almost all night!

At dawn the next morning, I raced into the living room behind my brothers. I stopped in my tracks, eyes sparkling with unshed tears. There, to greet me, was a beautiful new mahogany piano with a huge red bow tied around the piano bench! Beyond the piano, Mark chased the darling little Collie puppy all around the room, laughing happily. Mom sat with our baby sister, Lisa, who was overjoyed with her new rocking horse, and my other brother, Craig, was busy opening the toy arcade game he had asked Santa for. And through it all, Dad zoomed in and out with his slide camera, preserving the moment forever.

I looked around the room and smiled contentedly—no family could have been happier than ours was that morning.

I still treasure the piano, and always will. Not because it's an expensive make or style—it's a simple spinet and needs tuning often—but because each time I sit down to play, without fail, I am reminded of Christmas Eve 1960. And in the space of one single, solitary heartbeat, I have returned to the home I shared with my two brothers, a baby sister, and my parents so long ago. Lost in my memory, the snow falls down gently outside my bedroom window and I cough loudly to cover up the sound of a puppy whining. And then I hear it and my heart leaps for joy—the faint yet unmistakable sound of one piano key being struck in the middle of the night.

A Christmas Aha!

BY CHARLENE A. DERBY

Rose Mary, Millie, and I burst through the kitchen door with our parcels, flushed from the winter air and the excitement of the season. As the three older girls, we were inseparable. Earlier that day, we'd planned our own Christmas shopping trip, gotten permission to use the family car, and left nine-year-old Debbie to help Mom with Christmas decorations. But Debbie couldn't stand the suspense.

"What did you get me for Christmas?" she demanded.

"Nothing," we replied, catching our breath and setting our bags on the kitchen table. "These gifts are for Mom and Dad. Yours are coming from Santa Claus."

"I don't believe you," she huffed, folding her arms and staring us down.

"Why don't you ask Mom if you can help her with something?" we suggested, ignoring the fact that she'd been "help-ing" all morning. We continued to whisper conspiratorially while removing our coats and boots, reluctant to share our holiday secrets with our baby sister.

Later that day, Millie and I made plans to wrap gifts and put them under the tree. We smuggled wrapping paper, rib-bon, and bulky shopping bags into our parent's bedroom so we could work on the comfort of their queen-sized bed. We chatted cheerfully as we measured and cut the colored paper. When we got to Debbie's gift, we heard a loud "Aha!" from behind the closet door. With dismay, we realized that Debbie had heard everything.

We hadn't taken into consideration the fact that Mom and Dad's walk-in closet also opened from the sewing room. Debbie had outwitted us by coming in through the other door. To maintain our superiority, we had to think fast. After shooing her from the closet, Millie and I came up with a practical joke that we would carry out on Christmas morning.

When it was time to distribute the presents, Debbie eagerly reached for her gift. "I know what this is," she announced. "I heard you wrapping it." But when she opened the box, it was stuffed with Christmas bows.

"We thought you could use those to decorate your room," I explained.

"Yes," Rose Mary chimed in. "We couldn't afford an expensive gift. We've started to save for college."

Debbie set the bows aside and glared at us. "Where's my real gift?" she demanded. "I know you guys got me a real gift."

Millie reached under the tree skirt and pulled out another package. "Here it is," she said, "but don't spy on us again."

"Aha!" Debbie said as she tore the paper from her gift. From the look in her eyes, we could almost see the wheels turning. It seemed Debbie was making some plans of her own.

The following Christmas, Debbie didn't spy on us. She was busy in her own room, wrapping and singing carols to herself. She'd come to the kitchen for a freshly baked cookie or a piece of fudge, then returned to her work with a smug look on her face. She soon emerged with an armful of gifts, which she arranged happily under the tree. Then, she innocently asked us if we wanted to play a board game. We were pleased to see that she'd joined the tradition of sisterly gift giving.

But when I opened my gift from Debbie on Christmas morning, I saw that it was an empty perfume bottle. Thinking she might have made a mistake, I set it aside, intending to ask her about it later. Then I saw that Rose Mary and Millie had empty perfume bottles, too. I wondered if these bottles were all that Debbie could find to use as gifts.

"Debbie," I whispered as we set our gifts aside and headed toward the dining room with its tempting aromas of a traditional family dinner, "did you realize these bottles were empty?"

"Aha!" she exclaimed triumphantly. "I didn't have much money to spend on gifts. I'm saving for a new doll. I thought the bottles were pretty enough to use as decorations on your dressers!"

After a good laugh, Rose Mary, Millie, and I had an "Aha!" of our own. We should have known Debbie would think of a clever comeback for last year's trick gift. She was one of us, wasn't she? That Christmas, we stopped thinking of her as our baby sister, and allowed her to join our sophisticated sisterly sorority. From then on, we called ourselves the fearsome foursome and shared everything—apparently even our thoughts, for many Christmases ended with each of us purchasing the same item to give to the others. There was the year of the hand lotion, the year we all received bath puffs, and then the year we all ended up purchasing potholders.

But of all the wonderful Christmases we shared, none of us hold one more dear than the "Christmas aha!" year when our youngest sister joined the sisterly ranks and we became the fearsome four!

A Special Christmas Card

BY DOROTHY BAUGHMAN

"**B**ut, Mother . . . I can't."

My mother glanced at me sharply. "No buts. I want you to help me serve for my club meeting this afternoon, and I need some help tomorrow picking up the used toys for the needy children."

My mouth dropped open. "Oh, for . . . I don't want to spend the afternoon with a bunch of old women at a club meeting!"

"That will be enough, Dorothy," she said, her eyebrows rising into twin arches. "And you *will* help me tomorrow."

I threw my hands up in despair. "I'll have to call Joey and tell him I can't work on the posters for the dance until tomorrow afternoon."

She shrugged. "You have plenty of time for posters, but we have to finish getting the toys ready."

"Toys!" I snorted in disgust.

"Dorothy," said my mother quietly, "I know you have other interests now that you're growing up. But don't forget, you liked toys only a few years ago and looked forward to Santa."

Realizing she was right, I frowned. "I'm sorry, Mom." Though I apologized, I was still angry about my plans being ruined, and later that evening I was barely civil to the ladies.

"How's school, Dorothy?" Mrs. Dopson asked.

"Just fine, Mrs. Minnie," I answered absently.

"You certainly have grown into a fine young lady," said the elderly woman.

"Thank you," I said, surprised and a little ashamed by the woman's kind remark when it was obvious I was being rude.

After the meeting, my mother shot me a disappointed look. "Mrs. Dopson is a fine person, and a good friend. I'd like you to be nice to her."

"Yes, Ma'am," I muttered.

The next day, as I got ready to draw the posters for the dance, I couldn't find the markers I had originally planned on using. Thinking quickly, I remembered a set of watercolor pencils my father used to have.

"Mom," I shouted, "where are those watercolor pencils Daddy used to have?"

"In the desk," came her muted reply.

I turned to my father's desk and tugged open the first drawer. Dad had passed away nearly a year ago, and the desk had never been cleaned out. It was stuffed with old papers and odds and ends. As I pawed through everything, an envelope at the bottom of the stack caught my attention. The postmark was five years old.

Curious, I opened the envelope and pulled out a Christmas card. I skimmed the typed verse, and was about to toss it, when the fine script at the bottom of the card jumped out at me. I read the phrase silently. Stunned, I read it aloud.

Don't worry about the little girl's Christmas.
Minnie Dopson.

My mind flew back to Christmas five years past. The flashes of conversation between my parents had not meant much at the time. Father hadn't had a job in a while, and Mother had been worried about Christmas. I hadn't thought much about it since, because that was one of the best Christmases I'd ever had. There were so many toys . . .

Just then, my mother walked into the room. Seeing my tear-filled eyes, concern etched her face.

"Dorothy, what's the matter?"

With a trembling hand, I held the card up. She recognized it immediately.

"Oh, honey, I never meant for you to see this."

"We were broke, weren't we?" I asked, tears slipping down my face. "And Mrs. Dopson and the club arranged for my Christmas, didn't they? That's why I got so many toys that year."

Mother nodded. A bittersweet smile fluttered about her lips as she retold the story. "Your father had been out of work for over three months and we just didn't have any money for Christmas."

I wiped at my wet face. "Why didn't you tell me?" A new barrage of tears cascaded down my cheeks. "Oh! I've been so hateful to Mrs. Minnie!"

Mother shook her head. "Wouldn't it have made you feel worse knowing you had to be nice to her?" She glanced out the window and saw my friend, Joey, approaching.

"Here," she said handing me her handkerchief. "Dry your eyes."

As soon as Joey stepped into the room, he could see something was going on. He stopped in his tracks. "Have you been crying?"

"Not really," I said, as I wiped tears from my face. He frowned in bewilderment. I smiled at his confusion. "But I do have something to do before the posters are drawn," I said as I slid the card back into the desk drawer and closed it.

"Now what?" Joey asked, looking from me to Mother and back again.

I smiled and then turned to Mother. "Didn't I hear you say Mrs. Minnie was having trouble and couldn't walk to the market anymore?"

"Yes," Mother said, her smile growing. "She did mention something like that the other day."

I grabbed Joey's arm and pulled him toward the door. He frowned and looked back at my mother, begging her to explain. She merely grinned and waved as I marched him out.

"Joey," I said, feeling as though the Spirits of Christmas Past, Present, and Future had descended on me, "you and I are about to take a sweet old lady . . . I mean a sweet *elderly* lady, to market."

Joey looked at my beaming face and frowned suspiciously. "What's this all about, Dorothy?"

I tried to sniff back the tears, but couldn't. Through my watering eyes, I managed to smile, my voice breaking as I replied, "I have an overdue debt to pay."

A Gift of Love

BY BESS ANTISDALE

I clutched Annie, my Christmas baby doll, close to my heart and followed Mother down the long, cold hospital corridor. I already knew what I was going to do when I reached the hospital room where my cousin rested, which is why the pit of my stomach gurgled in objection. Mother had said so often, "When you give a part of yourself, expecting nothing in return, you'll know you have truly given a gift of love."

I knew what I would be doing would be a gift of love, so why was I so anxious?

Maybe it was because Annie and I were inseparable. I had waited so long for this delightfully soft dolly with a delicate, hand-painted porcelain head. Up until now, my doll family had looked like old-fashioned orphan children. Their bedraggled clothes hung loosely with missing buttons and faded colors. Most of my dolls were hand-me-downs from my older cousins. They were my family now, though, and I loved each one of them, and each one of them had been through a lot with me.

But Annie, my new doll, was extra special. She had been a dream come true the Christmas I turned six. I'd found her under the tree on Christmas morning in her pale pink dress, decorated with tiny, deeper-pink rosebuds along the collar, looking like a princess perched among the assortment of decorated gifts. I could tell by the way she looked at me that she had been waiting anxiously all night for me to pick her up in my arms and love her.

What must she think of me now that I had decided to give her away?

Very quickly, we had become the closest of friends. I didn't have a sister, so it was Annie who listened to my secrets. And she never teased me like my brothers did.

I lagged behind Mother, dragging my feet, aching with every step I took. My heart wanted to do the kind thing, but I struggled with the reality of my decision. It seemed as if time had slowed to a crawl as we moved down the hallway, past the patients in room after room. We finally walked into a starchy-white hospital room, and looked in at my cousin.

Edith had never been my favorite relative. In my opinion, she was always too bossy when we played together, and she always had much fancier things than the playthings and clothing I owned. Perhaps I was a little jealous; but today, following surgery, Edith looked pale and weak lying on the sterile white sheets and I felt sorry for her. I really did want to cheer her up.

Slowly, I removed Annie's soft, pink blanket. For a moment, I hesitated. Annie had been mine to hold for a short while, but she had already become so important to me. I wondered if she'd miss me. *Would she like Edith? Would she like Edith better than she had liked me?*

Mother stood near the end of the bed, her lips pursed as she watched.

"Here, Edith," I said as I moved in closer to the metal guardrails on the sides of her bed. "I want you to have Annie."

Edith struggled to sit up. Her eyes grew large as she looked at Annie. Then she reached out, ever so gently, and took my most prized possession.

"Oh, thank you so much," she said, her dull eyes sparkling again as she stroked the soft folds of Annie's pink dress. "I'll take good care of her."

I hoped so. I knew that she had recently dropped and broken her own porcelain doll, which was very similar to Annie. I also knew it would be rude to bring up something that might upset Edith, so I didn't dare mention it or give her any special instruction regarding *my* Annie. I had given Annie to her . . . what she now did with Annie was none of my business. Rather than say anything to incriminate myself, I whispered a faint goodbye to Annie, then quickly turned and rushed from the room without looking back.

My heart pounded madly in my tiny chest. I knew I had done the right thing. The way Edith's face shone with joy had been evidence of how much Annie had already helped in her recovery. But I couldn't stop the hot tears that scalded my cheeks and dripped onto the empty baby blanket I still held tightly. Mother joined me in the hall, hugging me for comfort. She knew how much giving Annie away had cost me. She understood my pain.

We padded noiselessly down the hospital halls that were accustomed to sharing grief. We descended the long brick stairway outside the hospital and were greeted by the early spring rain. The cold drops splashed on my cheeks, mingling with my tears. Before long, we had boarded the city bus and were seated behind the bus driver. As the bus chugged up Sunrise Boulevard, I felt as if a wide crack was forming between me and Annie, a crack that I was sure could never be sealed.

I had never felt so alone. Tenderly, I patted the forlorn baby blanket in my lap. Though it had been very hard, I knew that Jesus had helped me today to give a gift of love, and deep inside there was a spark of warmth in knowing I had done something special. But even deeper was a sadness that would not go away.

Mother's words, "Expecting nothing in return when you give" gripped my heart.

Over time, the hurt did seal over, but I never forgot Annie. I certainly never expected my empty arms to embrace another Annie. But, nearly fifty years later, God unexpectedly gave my heart's desire back to me.

Recently, while I examined a shelf filled with kitchen gadgets in the household section of a thrift shop, my wandering eyes spotted a beautiful doll all dressed up in her pink Sunday best. My heart skipped a beat and unexpected tears filled my eyes as I gazed, at long last, at the very same Annie doll I had given to my cousin so many years ago. Her wavy auburn hair framed a delicate blushing face, just as the hair on my Annie had.

Someone had placed a brand-new replica of *my* Annie in the wrong section of the store. And there she perched—atop a pile of assorted muffin tins and cookie cutters—looking just exactly as I had seen her the first time, perched on top of Christmas presents beneath my Christmas tree so many years ago. As I looked at her, it was as if she winked, as if she knew all along that I had missed my Annie so much all these years.

With shaking fingers, I reached for her. Holding her close, I felt a small glow in my heart. It may sound silly to someone else, but to me it was as if God had decided it was time for Annie and me to find one another again, and seal the hurt for good.

I couldn't wait to take her home with me.

Now Annie lives with me again, right where she belongs, and right where she will remain forever.

My Long Brown Stockings

BY M. DeLoris Henscheid

Carefully, I removed the tissue paper from the life-sized baby doll, rubbed my hand lovingly over her rough, cracked head, and straightened the pink dress. "I can't believe you're seventy years old," I whispered, a smile touching my lips. "I still remember the lesson you taught me."

I gently placed her beneath the Christmas tree, then sat with closed eyes and welcomed the memories of another Christmas many years ago.

It was an early 1938 December morning when I stepped out of our little house in Idaho Falls to walk the six blocks to Hawthorne School, where I was in the first grade. Something was different; snow was still piled everywhere, but it was not as cold. The glorious sun was melting the snow, creating wonderful, slushy puddles everywhere. Puddles were on the sidewalks, in the street, even in the snow that looked like tiny, silver lakes floating in mountains of vanilla ice cream.

It was so much fun walking to school that morning; I even forgot about those itchy long johns and hated long brown stockings I wore. I splashed in the baby puddles on the sidewalks and swooshed through the giant puddles in the streets. I climbed up on the snowy mountain and stuck my feet way down into the soft, wet snow—as far down as they would go—clear to the top of my long brown stockings. Then I slipped and tumbled down, squealing in delight. All the way to school, my galoshes made happy, sloshing noises.

When I finally opened the heavy door of the school, the long hall was empty and quiet. I quickly tiptoed into the cloakroom, hung my wet outdoor clothes on the hook, then pulled off the galoshes and left them in a wet puddle on the floor. Peeking into the classroom, I saw Teacher busy taking attendance. I tried to slip into my seat without notice, but failed.

"Oh, you're here," Teacher said, looking up at me sharply. "Why so late?" As if to answer her own question, her eyes dropped from my face to my wet shoes and dripping long brown stockings.

Her eyebrows rose slightly. "Did you bring an extra pair of stockings?"

My tummy felt funny. I couldn't look at Teacher. My voice wouldn't work. I shook my head.

"I'm sorry, but you know the rules," Teacher said. "You cannot stay at school in wet clothes. You'll get sick. You have to go home and change."

Anger bubbled inside of me as I stomped down the school sidewalk, soaked to the skin. I didn't want to go home. I didn't want to change my clothes.

Suddenly, I heard a big, loud crashing noise. A huge machine was digging long holes in the ground nearby. As the giant dirt eater crawled forward, it took another bite and spit out the dirt to one side. Behind the mountains of dirt lay a long line of cement pipes, one after the other, like a huge gray snake.

As I stared at the pipes, I had an idea. The men were busy with the machine, so they didn't see me crawl into the big round tube. My back shivered when I sat on the cold cement, but I didn't let that stop me from my sneaky plan.

The wet stockings were hard to pull off. They clung to the soggy long johns and my sticky, cold feet, but I refused to give up. When they finally flipped free, I fell back, hitting my head against the pipe and scraping my hand on the rough cement. Tears burned and spilled down my cheeks, dripping off my shivering chin. It was hard for my numb fingers to turn the cold, wet stockings inside out, but somehow I managed. Then I huffed and puffed to get them back on my goose-bumpy legs.

I was tired and hungry when I tromped back into the school, but I smiled at my cleverness. I didn't feel quite so clever when Teacher met me in the cloakroom and asked, "Did you go home and change your stockings?"

"Y-Y-Yes," I stammered. "But Mama didn't have any clean clothes for me."

Teacher looked at me for a long time, then turned and left the room. When she came back, she bent over and whispered, "Your mama wants you to go home, now."

I ran home as fast as I could. Mama was waiting at the door for me. I threw my arms around her and a huge gush of tears splashed down my face.

Mama held me tight. "All right," she said as she patted my back. "Tell me what happened." When I finished telling my story, Mama told me to take the wet clothes off, go to bed and get warm, and think about what I should do to right my wrong.

Early the next morning, I got some paper and crayons out of the drawer, sat at the table, and drew a picture of me, with big tears, sitting in the cement pipe holding my long brown stockings. I wrote on the bottom:

DeR TECHR IM SORRE.

Then I took my picture to school and laid it on Teacher's desk. I knew my teacher would forgive me because that's what teachers do, but had my actions been seen farther away than the classroom?

Christmas was coming. I began to worry that Santa had seen me in the cement pipe turning my long brown stockings inside out. I could think of little else until Christmas Eve finally arrived. That night, I pinned my long brown stockings together with a big safety pin and hung them over a chair near our Christmas tree. The next morning, I jumped out of bed and ran to my stockings. Both stockings were hanging, lumpy and heavy. Quickly, I shook out the first one. There was an apple, an orange, a banana, nuts, and lots of candy.

"Goody!" I squealed.

Then I reached into the second stocking and pulled out lumps of coal. *Oh, no, Santa had seen me in the pipe.* Then I found a letter pinned on the stocking. It read:

> *Dear little friend,*
> *This is to help you remember to always be true.*
> *I know you are trying because I heard you tell*
> *Mama and Teacher you were sorry.*
> *Thank you for being a brave girl.*
> *Now, look under the Christmas tree.*
> *Love Santa*

I ran to the tree and there sat my beautiful doll. And right next to her, folded neatly, were three new pairs of long brown stockings!

Grandpa Will's Gift

BY NELIA J. GREER

I do not remember receiving much individual attention from my grandfather. He tended to be an unassuming man, who preferred to sit quietly amid the commotion of family gatherings. But in 1937, the year I was five years old, Nebraska's capricious weather presented us with a "white" Christmas that led to a beautiful moment of understanding and joy between the youngest in the family and the eldest.

Times were hard during those Depression years, and simple pleasures were defined by frequent family gatherings, where plain food was served with love and gifts from the heart provided the sustenance to persevere. Snow covered the ground as my father's large extended family drew together at the home of my grandparents, as was the custom on that special day. Cheerful greetings and the aroma of good food greeted us, as family after family entered through the back door.

All brought gifts, and carried them to the living room where the Christmas tree, decorated primarily with handmade ornaments, stood in the recess of a bay window. Most gifts under the tree were the work of loving hands as well. Among them were the soft toy balls Grandma Belle made out of left-over yarn, ranging in size from tennis ball to that of a softball. Crocheted covers, resembling cupped doilies, provided child- and house-safe gifts to each of those youngsters she held close to her heart.

The round oak table in the dining room had been extended to its ultimate length, covered with snowy-white linen, and dressed with the best china and silver. When all was ready for the noon meal, the platters and bowls of food for an abundant Christmas feast were carried in. Grouped around the table, each standing behind their assigned chair, everyone joined in the traditional family blessing.

While the adults seated themselves, we children were ush- ered to the kitchen table, similarly provisioned. Seated on youth chairs or boosted with pillows, and babies in high chairs, we didn't mind being separated from parental watchdogs. There, under the gentle supervision of our youngest aunt, Aunt Harriet, we conversed spontaneously and laughed uproariously at our childish witticisms as we feasted on chicken and dumplings, Grandma Belle's customary main course for Christmas dinner.

At the meal's conclusion, Aunt Harriet and Aunt Alida began to shepherd us into the far bedroom.

"Come along," said Aunt Alida. "There's a big surprise waiting for you outdoors, and you must be dressed warmly!"

Our curiosity piqued, as we all wondered aloud at this unusual activity. Finally, when all were sufficiently swathed against the cold, Aunt Harriet directed, "Hush now, and fol- low me."

So anxious were we, we were right on her heels as she led us through living room, dining room, and kitchen. A little "push and hurry up" soon had us out the back door and down the steps. There, at the gate beyond the fenced yard, we spot- ted Grandpa Will with a horse and sled! Grandpa was dressed in his heavy barn jacket and cap with earflaps. He waved a mittened hand as we approached.

"Come along, we're going for a sleigh ride!" he called cheerfully. This was his domain, in which he was clearly in charge, and loving every minute.

Down the walk and through the gate we ran, clamoring aboard the sled's small four-by-six foot, blanket-covered, rough lumber top. Because the deck was fastened to metal runners the height of wagon wheels, Aunt Harriet had to help some of the littlest of the bunch. The sled's common use was to haul hay to the livestock when snow covered the ground. It surely wasn't fancy, but my cousins and I were so thrilled at the prospect of a sleigh ride with Grandpa, you would have thought it the counterpart of Santa's conveyance!

Soon all six of us were arranged on the sled—laughing and chattering, and filled with excitement. When Grandpa turned to see if we were ready to go, I noticed a little smile curving the corners of his mouth and a twinkle in his light blue eyes. I smiled back, happy to be sharing this moment with him.

"Hold on now," advised our proud grandfather. There were no seats or even a handrail to grasp, so we sat with thick mittens clinging to the deck edges and to each other.

"Giddy-up, Lady."

Lady, a plow horse unused to human cargo was a little hesitant at first, but under Grandpa's calm guiding hand, she soon settled into a rhythmic trot, and the sleigh bells Grandpa had appended to her harness began to jingle merrily. One cannot imagine if Lady had feelings of privilege or felt put-upon for this duty, but clearly she was Grandpa's choice for this day's jaunt, and I like to think she felt as proud of Grandpa.

We were momentarily silenced by this new experience, as we traversed the half-mile to town and back. Clouds above threatened more snow, but that didn't dampen our spirits as we began to get into the adventure and sang "Jingle Bells" at the top of our lungs. We called out "Merry Christmas!" to everyone we saw. Here and there, we glided past youngsters braving the cold to try out a new Christmas sled or attempting to roll the powdery snow into the rounded segments of a snowman.

In less than an hour, we were returned to the homestead and deposited at the gate, chilled through and through, but exuberant from the thrill of our excursion.

I must admit to a slight feeling of superiority at a surmised envy on the part of those children we saw on the street. I realize a homemade utility sled is of lowly origin and intended only to serve a practical purpose; it was Grandpa Will's desire to do something special—within his realm—for his grandchildren that made us feel privileged. Even at that tender age, I understood and appreciated his gift.

Sometimes Less Is More

BY BARBARA JEANNE FISHER

As a five-year-old child, I was a coward at heart. I remember so well how excited I was that Santa was coming and bringing us something special, and how I reacted when he finally arrived. True to character, the minute Santa knocked on the door, I screamed, "I have to go potty!" and ran to the bathroom to hide. Somehow, Mom managed to get me into the living room, where Santa gave me a rubber baby doll, but all the coaxing in the world didn't get me on his lap.

Instead, my sweet baby brother, Bernie, was lifted to the place of honor, smiling and cooing. As soon as Santa put Bernie down, however, Bernie picked up my new baby doll. The doll was my one gift and I was frantic he'd harm her in some way. I quickly grabbed the doll by the feet—begging Bernie to let go of the doll's head. He wouldn't. With a whoosh and a splash of tiny white foam balls, I was left holding the doll's body, while her head rolled across the floor. I was crushed, but in her magic way, Mom somehow managed to stuff most of the foam balls back into my baby doll, *and* twist her forlorn head back on.

My sister, four years older than I, was last to sit on Santa's lap. JoAnne feared if she didn't believe in Santa, she wouldn't get a present. She played the "perfect child" role all the way to the end, thrilled with the miniature sewing machine she received. I watched in amazement as JoAnne sat there hugging and kissing Santa for several minutes. Mom and Dad were so proud of her!

But later, when Santa was saying goodbye, JoAnne ran back to him, hugged him tightly once more, and whispered, "Good job! Goodbye, Uncle Urbie."

When Christmas came the following year, I was braver, but it didn't matter—my siblings and I all had the mumps. Santa wouldn't be making an appearance in our house this year. To make matters worse, Dad had gotten a bonus and announced he'd purchased a very nice gift for us to share. He was very upset that we were all sick, especially on Christmas.

You can't imagine our surprise on Christmas morning when we scooted from our sick beds to see our presents. When we walked into our huge farmhouse living room, we found a gym set waiting for us, complete with a slide and swings!

Dad had stayed up late on Christmas Eve to assemble it—right in the house—just to cheer us up! We were the only children we ever knew who had a gym set in their living room! Despite the mumps, we enjoyed swinging and sliding all day long, and Mom and Dad enjoyed watching us!

But that was the fifties. Rather than a handful of gifts, more thought went into one special gift. Reflecting on my childhood, I believe families back then were closer. Going to church to celebrate the birth of Christ always came before parties and presents, and because sometimes we received only one gift, we learned to share. We also learned that sometimes less was quite a bit more, and even when the gifts were less than we had hoped for, we knew—no matter what—that we were always loved.

At the Five and Dime

BY ARTHUR BOWLER

O nce upon a time, there were no malls. At Christmastime, you were forced to search for treasures in the stores of a large city or in the Mom and Pop shops on Main Street. I spent many afternoons roaming through Peterson's Five and Dime downtown. It had everything from candy to sewing accessories to snow shovels, but shopping there was not easy. It was known as "Grouch Peterson" in honor of its unfriendly proprietor, whose favorite expressions were "Don't touch that!" and "You break it, you take it."

The store was dark and dusty and the wooden floor creaked as you walked through the aisles. This made it easier for Peterson to keep his eye on your every move over his half glasses, as if he suspected you were about to steal something. He was the owner and the only employee. If you had a question or, God forbid, a complaint or a return, you had to deal with him. He was not a popular man in town, and I suspect he knew it. There were seldom any sales in those days, and certainly never with Grouch Peterson.

Yet, in 1961, in a town with just a handful of businesses, there weren't too many choices for an eleven-year-old boy to find a Christmas present for his mother. Peterson's was it, and one day in December, I got a glimpse at the real Peterson, and he surprised me.

Snow had been falling heavily for hours, and it looked like school would be cancelled the next day. Long before the sun set that afternoon, the streets were bare. People had gone home early to avoid being stuck in the storm. Peterson lived alone above the store, so getting home was no problem for him. As I entered, I found neither customers nor Peterson himself. Back then, there was no music in stores, and the shop was dead quiet except for the occasional rumble of a snow-plow as it made its way down Main Street. I started wandering through the aisles, feet creaking on the floorboards. When Peterson emerged quietly from the back room, it appeared— even to my eleven-year-old eyes—that he had been crying.

"Hello, Mr. Peterson," I said quietly. There was no response, just a short wave of the hand. "Looks bad out there," I mut-tered, searching for some kind of conversation.

"Um," he answered.

He was holding a piece of paper in his hand. In unusual frankness, he explained that he was going to be alone for Christmas. A widower with only one child, his daughter, who lived abroad, had written him a letter—the only reliable form of communication from overseas—to say that she would not be able to make it home for the holiday. It was too much for Grouch Peterson, and for me.

For many years, I had seen Peterson as a cranky old man, to be avoided and made fun of. Now, I felt sorry for him.

Without a second thought, I looked him straight in the eye and said, "Mr. Peterson, why don't you come to my dad's church on Christmas Eve? It'll be real pretty, with lots of candles and nice songs, and afterwards a few people always come to our house for something to eat and to be together for a while. Why don't you come, too?"

Peterson stared at me with a blank expression. The light of a passing snowplow flashed across his chiseled face, wrinkled from years of work and loneliness. Our eyes locked, and after a moment of silence that stretched into what seemed like forever, he finally answered.

"Well, maybe I will," he said with the hint of a smile.

And so, among the faithful at the candlelight Christmas service, there was a surprising new visitor, a man who had cried out for one of the most basic of human needs. Although I felt really good about what I had done and I never looked at Peterson as a grouch again, it wasn't until I was a grown man that I recognized that simple act for what it was. When I did, tears pooled in my eyes and a feeling of pride for the little boy who had walked into Peterson's store that afternoon and offered friendship to a grouchy old man poured from me. And as I wiped my eyes, I felt prouder still of the grouchy old man who was able to accept that friendship for what it was.

Santa Is Real

BY JO E. GRAY

The nation was at war with Germany the year I was in fourth grade. My father was working as a civilian on a naval base far from our North Texas home. As Christmas approached, my four brothers and I kept our fingers crossed and added one new line to our nightly prayers, "Please bring Daddy home for Christmas."

Life on the farm that winter didn't provide much time for idleness; we were kept busy with school and chores. Living on a farm had some luxuries—we didn't go hungry. We had a couple of cows that provided milk and butter, and chickens were kept as a source of eggs and as Sunday dinner, which was shared with the circuit minister or the spinster teacher who was given housing with another neighbor.

Even though the war brought food rationing, we knew there would be a homemade cake topped high with cara-mel frosting because the neighbors often gave their rationing stamps to Momma to help her provide for her growing fam-ily, and Momma knew how to make things stretch. Her talent became obvious as worn pants were mended and handed down to the next child in line. When clothing had no life left, they were made into strips, braided, and turned into rugs for added warmth on cold linoleum floors.

Life went on much the same during the long months Daddy was away. The chores still had to be done on a daily basis, and the winter days brought a constant demand for firewood to keep the house heated. There were still eggs to be collected, animals to be fed, and we still had to do the most demanding of all chores—milking the cows every morning and every evening, every day of the year.

The one thing we all had to look forward to during those short, cold winter days was Christmas. It meant the annual Christmas production at school, followed by an appearance by Santa. Every child who attended school would have a part in the pageant, and every family would hurry through the chores in order to attend the evening event. This year was no different. Santa came into the building on cue. Every child received a red stocking containing a shining red apple, an orange, and a piece or two of hard ribbon candy.

After Santa's visit, families bundled up, hugged their friends, and promised to visit during the holidays. Then, carrying tired young children, everyone made their way back home, some traveling several miles on foot while others were fortunate enough to have automobiles and enough rationing stamps to keep the cars outfitted with rubber tires and gasoline.

As we trudged home through the crunchy snow, I wondered how we would celebrate Christmas in our customary fashion while trying to pretend everything was normal. There would be a Christmas tree standing in the corner of our living room, as far away from the wood-burning stove as possible, and like the previous years, it would be decorated with paper chains of red and green construction paper held together with flour and water glue. The tree would be a small cedar, cut from our 180-acre farm. The only real difference was that without Daddy, my brothers and I would have to select the tree and haul it home alone.

One trip into town provided all the Christmas shopping we would do. Gifts were bought at the Five and Dime from proceeds earned from collecting pecans in the creek bed. Trying to keep the purchased items hidden from one another added to the thrill of having picked the gifts out without adult help. We each chipped in for a special gift for Momma—a gift that was always selected by the oldest brother. I still recall the bottles of toilet water and pastel-colored boxes of bath powder that were carefully opened on Christmas morning and the big smile and sincere thank-you hug for each of us.

Of course, Santa Claus would still come to those who believed. I wanted desperately to believe, even though the kids in my class had made fun of me as I fought to defend my innocence. In order to test my faith, I prayed. I was convinced that if Santa granted me a special wish, I'd know for sure he was real. I agreed to forget about the doll with white boots and long dark curls as pictured in the Sears & Roebuck catalogue, if only Daddy would be home for Christmas.

"I want just one thing," I whispered each evening as I knelt beside my bed. "If you are real Santa, bring Daddy home for Christmas."

A week before Christmas, however, we children were told that Daddy wouldn't be with us this year. The trip was too far and gasoline was another rationed item. But regardless of Momma's words, I continued to secretly wish for Santa to bring Daddy home.

Neighbors stopped by to exchange Christmas wishes. An out-of-town aunt arrived with gifts for each of us: spinning wooden tops for my brothers, and, for me, a baby doll that was capable of drinking and wetting. The doll with painted hair brought some gladness to my disappointment, but I couldn't accept the fact that we were going to celebrate Christmas without Daddy. *Who would get up early and start the fire?* It just felt wrong to be happy.

I stayed in my bedroom most of the time. I had no desire to join in festivities that seemed meaningless. After all, if Santa was not real, then my only hope of seeing Daddy on Christmas morning would never come true. My older brothers seemed resigned to the fact that Daddy wouldn't be with us on Christmas. They teased that I was a baby to believe in Santa.

Before going to sleep on Christmas Eve, I offered God and Santa one last desperate prayer, put my head under the covers, and cried myself to sleep.

The house was still cold when I awoke the next morning. Listening closely, I heard someone building a fire in the big potbelly stove. As I laid there, hoping upon hope that it was Daddy making the fire, hushed voices drifted through the thin walls of my bedroom and I heard a male voice.

I threw off the layer of heavy warm quilts and hurried across the cold linoleum floor to the adjoining living room.

"I knew it!" I shouted as I spotted Daddy beside the stove. With tears of joy streaming down my face, I raced across the room and threw my arms around him. "Oh, Daddy," I shouted to my surprised father. "Santa *is* real!"

Seeing Is Believing

BY PATSY THOMAS

C hristmas of 1951 will forever stand apart from the many other holidays I have had in my lifetime. At six years old, a subtle change occurred—a division of the two worlds I lived in. Up until that point, I had not questioned the magic of the Christmas season; however, this year was different. At the age of six, I was growing up, yet I had a treasure trove of remarkable fantasies in my young mind, and I wasn't ready to let go.

My father worked for the Frisco Railroad, which meant shift work. When Daddy was preparing to go to work at four o'clock that Christmas Eve afternoon, it began to snow—a rare occurrence in Enid, Oklahoma. I sat on the old-fashioned sofa, pressed my nose to the frosty glass panes of our living room window, and watched the white flakes float down from the sky. Daddy eased onto the couch to sit beside me.

I looked up at him, staring at the black patch that covered his left eye. The week before, he had been injured on the job and gotten a sliver of steel in his eye. My younger sister and brothers were afraid of the black patch, but I liked his pirate look. It reminded me of one of the characters from Robert Louis Stevenson's *Treasure Island,* a book Mama had recently read to me.

"Daddy, are you sure Santa will come?" I asked. "We don't have a chimney for him to bring the toys down."

Daddy ruffled my blonde curls and looked at me with a twinkle in his eye. "Don't worry, honey." He stood up from the sofa and lifted me into his arms. "When I get home at midnight, I'll be waiting for him at the front door to let him in."

Perfect! I should have known Daddy would think of everything! I gave Daddy a bear hug and he put me down, tweaking my nose. I watched him put on his coat and reach for his lunch pail. When Daddy leaned down to kiss Mama goodbye, my younger brothers and sister hid behind her dress, preparing for a morning ritual they loved. As soon as he had kissed Mama, he peeked around her and quickly shouted, "Boo!" Off the little ones ran to the bedroom, giggling all the way.

After supper and our baths, Mama began the evening ritual of tucking us in. We begged her for one more story, one more trip to the bathroom, and one more sip of water. We were all too excited to sleep. *How could we bear to wait until morning?* Being the oldest, I made constant trips to the living room to make sure all was ready. *Were the cookies and milk set out for Santa? What of the chopped carrots for the reindeer?*

Mama looked over her shoulder from where she sat on the sofa, hearing my unvoiced worries. "Patsy, Santa won't come with your presents if you don't get to sleep soon." Finally, she came to sit on the edge of my bed that I shared with my little sister, Kathy. We were snuggled deep under the covers, giggling.

"Mama, I hope Santa brings me the baby doll I asked for," I said with a big yawn.

"Me, too," Kathy added sleepily.

Mama smiled. "I'm sure you girls won't be disappointed."

The next thing I knew, Daddy and Mama were standing by the bed shaking me gently. "Come see what Santa has brought you!" Rubbing sleep from my eyes, I bounded from the bed and hurried toward the living room.

At the threshold, I stopped. The other kids pushed past me to sit beside Mama. They crowded around her on the floor near the tree. Daddy sat on the sofa watching me. As his one good eye met mine, he smiled and winked. I needn't have worried about Santa finding his way to us. My dad had met him at the door, just as he had promised.

The room was beautiful, aglow with Christmas magic. I could feel Santa's strong presence still lingering in the air. Everything I had ever imagined in my fantasy world was true and real. Nothing else could come near to the feeling of absolute wonderment I felt at that very moment.

Then, I saw something I had not expected—not even in my wildest dreams! An easel with a green chalkboard was propped next to the sofa. My eyes fixed on the board, reading a message printed only for me in colored chalk. "HOPE YOU HAVE A MERRY CHRISTMAS, PATSY. LOVE, SANTA."

"He's real!" I breathed.

The proof was right there in his printed words. Since my siblings were too young to read, I couldn't prove to them that Santa was real—nor did I realize there was no need to do so. It hadn't dawned on me that none of them had ever questioned or needed the evidence that I had suddenly required. But no more; my questions had all been answered! Caught up in that awesome moment, my faith was completely restored. Only one thing was missing—the sound I'd been listening for. Then there it was! I ran to the window and pressed my face to the pane. Sleigh bells!

The glistening snow was still falling, but through it I saw what my heart needed to see. High above the darkened streets a faint red light—Santa's sleigh!—was still visible in the early morning sky. I watched as the light faded out of sight, my little heart swollen with the knowledge that Santa really was real, and that my Dad had opened the door for him, just like he'd said he would.

Let There Be Light

BY EMMARIE LEHNICK

I ran the one block from school to my house, clutching the Santa cookie I got at my second grade Christmas party. Bounding onto the porch, I opened the front door, yelling, "Mama, I have a surprise!"

Mama sat in her rocker, making a rag rug in front of the open gas stove. December 1940 marked almost two years since she had been in the tuberculosis sanatorium. I could see by her flushed cheeks that she felt sick again today.

"Mama, look at this cookie!" I exclaimed. "My teacher and her mother baked Santa cookies for our party, but I didn't eat mine. I rewrapped it for you to see. When Ludie gets home, we can share it."

Mama carefully folded back the wax paper around the six-inch red and white decorated cookie. "Oh, my goodness! It's just perfect!"

"My teacher had a real Christmas tree in our room with lights and beautiful colored balls all over it. It was the prettiest tree I have ever seen," I exclaimed as I glanced up at the red and green paper rope that looped from corner to corner of the room, with a paper star hanging at the center crossing.

Mama's brown eyes followed mine. "After we lost the farm during the Depression, money has been kind of scarce, as you know. But next year," Mama straightened her back, jutting out her chin with determination, "we *will* have a tree with lights. Lots of lights. I promise."

When my sister, Ludie, came in from school, Mama divided the Santa cookie into three parts. Since it was my cookie, I got the head and one arm. We savored it, licking the icing until every bit was gone.

After eating an early supper, Papa, Mama, Ludie, and I dressed up in our best clothes and walked the seven blocks to our church. We walked everywhere because we didn't have a car. The crisp night air numbed my nose and stung my cheeks. Most of the churches in our little town held their Christmas programs on the same night, so we had lots of company on the walk.

Mom chose a seat at the back of the church, which gave me a fright. *What if I couldn't see Santa from here?* I knew he would show up at the end of the service, but he always stayed at the front of the church. I shouldn't have worried. I heard the jingling of bells first, then Santa came in from the back of the auditorium and dashed right past me, carrying a big, red bulging sack! It happened so fast, at first I wasn't sure. But when Papa let me stand up in the seat so I could see better, I knew I had seen right. And what I had seen was very confusing.

This Santa was tall and skinny, his suit was red cotton, and his beard looked scraggly.

Unnerved, and a bit put out as well, I whispered in Mama's ear, "He's not Santa." I glanced at Santa again to be sure and then added, "The real Santa looks like the Coca-Cola pictures of him in the grocery store."

A small frown played about Mamma's forehead as she caught Papa's eye and replied, equally quiet, "This is Santa's helper. The real Santa is in his workshop getting everything ready for Christmas." I looked at her solemnly, accepting her words as I knew I should, despite the small fear of doubt that had crept into my mind.

I turned back to the front of the church and watched as Santa's helper called out names. Kids, hearing their names, raced to the front to get their presents. When he called my sister's name, she almost knocked me off the seat in her rush to get her present. I waited and waited, concerned Santa's helper had some powers after all and had decided I was ineligible for a gift because he knew I knew he wasn't real.

"He doesn't have a present for me," I lamented as I searched my parents' faces.

Just then, a booming voice called, "Emmarie Turner!"

I caught my breath, jumped down from the seat, and ran to the front. The Santa's helper handed me a Miss America coloring book and a drawstring sack of jacks. Then he gave me a bag filled with an orange, an apple, and ribbon candy. I recognized the ring on Santa's helper's finger, and for a moment stood stock-still. Santa's helper was Mr. Allred, the man who did magic tricks for us kids. I looked up at him in awe. He was the perfect Santa's helper because the kids loved him and he loved kids!

Clutching my presents, I turned and started back down the aisle. For a minute, fright overtook me. I couldn't remember where my family was sitting. Just before panic set in, Mama stepped out into the aisle.

I hurried to her.

She smiled at my loot. "Those are nice presents."

Grateful to be back with my own family, I looked up into her smiling eyes. "I can color a picture for you."

Stars filled the sky dome above us as we walked home. Mama held one of my hands; my other hand was busy hugging my presents close to me. When we got home, Papa lit the stove while we shucked our coats. Mama sliced an orange into four pieces. Each of us took a piece and let the sweet juice delight our mouths.

Christmas meant fresh fruit, which was a real treat for us. Santa always gave us fruit and nuts for our Christmas morning gifts. On Christmas Eve, after we ate supper and did the dishes, Papa stepped out to the back porch and Mama struggled with a cardboard box under her bed.

"Girls, close your eyes real tight," Mama instructed.

Giggling in anticipation, Ludie and I squeezed our eyes and covered our faces with our hands.

"Okay. You can look now," Mama said.

I gasped with delight as Mama handed me my doll wearing a new pink dress. I recognized the material that was scraps left from my summer Sunday dress. Ludie's doll had a new pink dress, too.

"Thank you, Mama," Ludie and I cried as we hugged her tightly. Then Papa brought out a table, a small chair, and a larger chair. This furniture, made from wood scraps and extra-heavy cardboard, fit Ludie and me exactly! We could sit and color and play at this table in total comfort.

"This is the best Christmas I've ever had," I said as I perched on my new chair. I knew that Papa and Mama worked many nights making our presents after we had gone to bed. Hugging my doll, I twirled around the room on the worn rose-patterned linoleum.

"My feet want to dance," I said. "I'll bet I had the best Christmas of anyone in the whole world!"

Mama's eyes filled with tears. "Yes," she said, "we are truly blessed."

That Christmas was Mama's last Christmas.

In August, while cleaning out Mama's dresser drawers, we found—hidden under her gowns—two tissue-wrapped presents with tags: FOR LUDIE, WITH LOVE, MAMA and FOR EMMARIE, WITH LOVE, MAMA.

Inside the tissue were two blue doll dresses lovingly made and perfect. Also in the drawer were two boxes of colored lights from an after-Christmas sale. Just as Mama had promised, our next Christmas tree would have lots of lights.

Burnt Toast and Tinsel

BY BARBARA KIFFIN

'Twas the Night Before Christmas in the Year of Our Lord 1932. 'Twas also still very dark as three-year-old me lay nestled, all snug in my bed, dreaming of sugarplums, when—just as dawn was breaking over Greenland—my eight-year-old brother, Rex, the "Ghost of Christmas Yet to Come" crept into my frigid chamber.

"Wake up, Bip," he whispered. "I heard the reindeer on the roof and Santa Ho-Ho-Hoing, but I waited ere they drove out of sight." Truly, my brother was steeped in Clement C. Moore. "Wake up," he shouted into my ear. After another minute, he pleaded again, "Please wake up, Bip."

Finally, I complied. The hot water bottle had grown cold anyway. As I rubbed my sleepy eyes, Rex dragged my slippers from under the bed and tossed my bathrobe over my head, stuffing my spaghetti arms into the sleeves.

Then, as quietly as we could, we tippy-toed downstairs for breakfast. This stealth grew from the orders laid down by the Queen of the Kitchen and the King of the Forest: Not one present was to be shaken, ripped open, or even touched until both of us had eaten our breakfast.

No doubt, had they not said both, we wouldn't have had our joint adventure; Rex would have gone solo.

For a week, Rex had been in a frenzy of activity, and all day Christmas Eve he was a living itch! Never before was the ritual of the tree performed with such speed. This ritual called for us to leave the Queen of the Kitchen in peace to make cookies. Our role was to help the King of the Forest pick out two of nature's mistakes for transformation into a glorious tree of wondrous symmetry. Every year, our father played one-upmanship with Mother Nature. That's why Mum had dubbed him King of the Forest. And if you'd ever tasted Mum's cookies, you'd know why she was Queen of the Kitchen!

Choosing the tree was the least of it. We knew that even if a cheap tree looked a little scrawny, Daddy would bring it to beauty by the addition of branches God might have forgotten.

Daddy had a method: He bought two cheap trees for less than the price of a respectable one, denuded the skimpier of the two, drilled holes in the trunk of the survivor, and filled in where old Mother Nature had been sloppy. It was amazing; each year he built a whispering pine worthy of last year's tinsel!

Yes, we saved tinsel.

Tinsel, the Christmas tree's thin, glory-long, flexible strips of silver, which, when hung with care, were delicate cascades of icicles, sparkling against the tree's multicolored lights and were the most beautiful things on the tree. Tinsel was a lead product, which accounted for its softness and drape-ability. It's a wonder we weren't all dead by New Year's.

Tinsel was quite beautiful when applied artistically, one strand at a time. Dad removed it at the end of the holiday with the same great care and saved it on the notched cardboard it came on.

Before tinsel ever touched the tree, though, the lights were strung. The lights, too, were magnificent, but these strings of color faded to black if just one bulb was dead. Dependable strings of miniature white lights that stayed on—even if one light was missing—hadn't been invented yet. If the lights passed floor testing, great sighs of relief echoed through the halls of our house. Failure meant we had to unscrew the bulbs, one by one, to weed out the duds and replace them so the whole string would work again. This caused God's rival in forestry to color the air with words it was best children not hear. When, at last, the lights had been carefully wound through Daddy's and God's boughs, the Queen would step into the room to view the masterpiece.

Without fail, the Queen found something amiss. "Oh, Frank," she murmured, "there are three blue ones in a row."

Uh, oh! More colored air!

Next came the ornaments, which could be handled only by the King and Queen because they were made of delicate glass—fine and oh-so fragile. Rex and I stood by and watched in wonder. For the finale, I—the littlest child—was lifted by our frazzled father to place the once-beautiful angel atop the magnificent creation. She was a little tacky and shopworn, but she was my angel and I loved her dearly.

After a hearty meal of Welsh Rarebit, Rex and I were bundled off to bed. I was all tuckered out and asleep in heavenly peace in no time, but my brother, the heir, had trouble coming down from the eight-day trip of anticipation he'd been floating around on. When he shouted that first "Wake up, Bip!" it was four in the morning and dawn was far from breaking over Hasbrouck Heights, New Jersey.

Rex wasn't skilled in hand-squeezing oranges, and frozen juice hadn't been invented yet, but he could handle a glass of milk. And he was bold enough to make toast. Toast, in 1932, was bread electrified. Automatic, pop-up toasters hadn't been invented yet, either. Toasters were dangerous, little, A-frame contraptions with flip-down sides. Bread was crisped by naked electric coils at the center, one side at a time. Buttering toast was another challenge. Even when butter was at room temperature, it wasn't much better than the outside temperature.

But, since God helps those who help themselves, Rex helped himself and me to Christmas breakfast. Then Rex helped himself to whatever had his name on it. Thanks to a whimsical mother, tags were signed by Santa, Old Nick, and Sandy Claws.

In perfect clarity, I recall watching Rex tear the paper from an Erector Set, a stamp album, lead soldiers, and the *Boys Book of Adventure*. But I haven't the faintest memory of what the jolly old elf brought me that Christmas, nor do I recall what the King and Queen thought of our adventure when they awoke. I was still in shock at having been woken when dawn was breaking over Greenland!

A Million Stars Looked Down

by Jewell Johnson

"Time to get your coats on," Mom called to my two brothers and me on Christmas Day. "Dad's got the car warmed up."

White steam billowed from the tailpipe as I tumbled into the backseat with my brothers, Deisel and Gary. We were going to celebrate Christmas Day at Uncle Oscar's farm, something we all enjoyed.

Soon, the prairie where we lived ended and skinny poplar trees and scrubby bushes dotted the snow-covered land. "We're in brush country now," Dad said, letting us know we'd passed the first leg of the journey. For the next half hour, we traveled down a bumpy, gravel road.

Suddenly, Mom pointed to a figure in the distance. "There's Oscar waiting for us!"

I knew by the sound of her voice that she was smiling, and I smiled, too, as I craned my neck to see my uncle. He wore a fur cap, the collar of his thick coat buttoned up to his chin. We hadn't seen him in a long time, and it felt good just to see him standing there beside a big sleigh pulled by two brown horses with long white manes.

"Goddog!" Uncle Oscar called as Dad opened the car door. That means "good day" in Swedish, which is the language Dad and Uncle Oscar had learned to speak as children.

High snowdrifts blocked the road to Uncle's farm, so we always left our car on the highway and rode to the farm on the sleigh. In my mind, the snowdrifts were part of the magic of the season; without them, we might not have gotten a wonderful sleigh ride.

"Duck your heads!" Uncle said as he spread the buffalo robe over Mom, my brothers, and me. "This will keep out the cold wind." Then, turning to Dad, he added, "John, you ride up front with me."

From beneath the warm robe, we heard Uncle yelp, "Gid up!" The horses' harnesses jingled merrily, the sleigh jerked, and we glided over the snow. My mind raced ahead to the farmhouse where my cousins would be creating a wonderful meal, and my heart sang in rhythm with the horses' feet as we effortlessly sped across the wide-open spaces.

Almost too soon, I heard Uncle yell, "Whoa!" and felt the sleigh stop beside Uncle Oscar's small white house nestled among poplar trees and brush. When Dad pulled off the buffalo robe, my brothers and I popped out like gophers ready for whatever the holiday would bring. Mom laughed at our rosy faces—pink from the heat we had created and shared beneath the robe, not angry red like the faces of our father and Uncle Oscar, who had braved the biting wind.

"Come in! Come in!" Cousin Helen called from the porch, practically jigging in anticipation as she wiped her hands on her pink and green apron. The smell of turkey and sage wafted through the open door as we hurried inside.

"Get close to the stove to warm up," Helen advised, allowing us to spread our cold hands over the black kitchen range.

Uncle Oscar hung his hat up and turned to Dad. "It must have been twenty below zero this morning." Dad nodded as they stomped the snow from their overshoes. We children exchanged a knowing look and shared a quiet giggle. *The men were so predictable!* They always talked about the weather whenever they were together.

Within minutes of our arrival, Cousin Florence was placing a mail-order catalog on a chair for little Gary to sit on and calling everyone to dinner. Deisel and I sat on the piano bench.

Everything was delicious, and we all ate our fill. Later, while the ladies washed the dishes, the men went into the parlor and Uncle set up a game of chess. He and Dad sat close to the potbellied stove for the rest of the afternoon, challenging one another.

We children anxiously raced to the kitchen as soon as Florence called to say the table was cleared and it was time to play checkers. After checkers, we played prize bingo. I won a yellow pencil and Gary won a jigsaw puzzle.

At dusk, Florence took the glass chimney off the kerosene lamp, lit the wick, and set it back down on the table. A soft yellow glow filled the kitchen as we snacked on apple salad, cold turkey, and rolls, before it was time to go.

Reluctantly, we bundled up into coats and boots, and headed back outside. I loved coming to visit Uncle Oscar and his family as much as I hated leaving. But I knew one more secret bit of magic awaited me outside in the dark. Because the wind had died down, we no longer needed the buffalo robe, and this time I could see the stars.

The sleigh runners squeaked on the hard snow, the horses' harnesses jingled, and I gazed into the sky. There were stars so near it seemed I could touch them, and stars so far away they were only dots in the sky.

"One, two, three, four," I counted.

"You can't count them all," my older and wiser brother said.

"I can too," I replied. "Five, six, seven . . ." When I got to fifty, I stopped. Deisel was right—there were too many stars to count. And every one of them was beautiful.

At the main road, the horses stopped and we quietly jumped off the sleigh.

"Thank you for the ride, Uncle," I said, and reached out to shake his hand. He smiled as he grasped my hand, then he looked at Dad.

"Thanks a million," Dad said in Swedish. Uncle Oscar nodded.

My brothers and I snuggled together in the backseat of the car as Dad roared the motor to life. When the car jerked forward, I peered up at the stars one more time and thought about Dad's parting words to his brother.

Snuggling closer to Deisel and Gary, I whispered, "I like everything about Christmas Day at Uncle Oscar's. Best of all, I like the sleigh ride in the night when a million stars look down on me."

Boy to the World!

BY CAROLINE B. POSER

"How was your weekend?" Kathy, my son Griffin's day-care office manager, asked.

"Oh," I sighed. "Not that great." It was first thing Monday morning and I was dropping off my youngest. I had just left my older two boys, Mark and Daniel, at school.

Kathy raised her eyebrows.

I offered her a lopsided grin. "My children are like a small band of monkeys," I said, picturing my three sons, all under the age of six.

"Oh, well . . . it's that time of year," she added.

"I suppose . . . " I said, not quite believing my words.

I was still recovering from the second weekend in Advent and prayed things would get better, not worse, as the holiday season approached. I had already arranged my work schedule and decreased my commitments in an effort to implement all the traditions I remembered from my own childhood, and I planned to enjoy the holiday season. But, so far, that wasn't happening.

I had envisioned the kids and I putting up the tree and decorating it during Thanksgiving weekend while listening to Christmas music. Then, over the course of the next several weeks, we'd bake cookies, make peppermint bark, and bake other goodies together, including the customary gingerbread houses. We'd talk about the birth of Jesus while we set up our nativity scene under the tree. We'd watch Christmas movies, make wish lists for Santa, and observe Advent *every* Sunday. That meant I'd have to plan a lesson and an activity and a treat, but that would be okay. After all, I was only working four-day weeks in December. I figured we could count down the days with our Advent calendar. I thought it would be fun. Yeah, right.

What it was really like in my house was far from the pleasant scene from a Norman Rockwell painting I had envisioned. Instead . . . *I* put up the tree. The boys lost interest in decorating it after hanging a few ornaments each, at which point they proceeded to use them as missiles and other weapons. A couple of weeks later, our tree's ornaments remained on the top half only—as does the tree of any family with an eighteen-month-old toddler. (Though, one day, I *did* find a pair of dirty socks draped across one of the lower branches.)

The boys would rather have watched superhero cartoon reruns than any of *my* favorite Christmas specials, like *Santa Claus is Comin' to Town, Rudolph the Red-Nosed Reindeer,* and *Frosty the Snowman.* I insisted that if they were to watch superhero cartoons, they'd have to do it upstairs and without me. They went gladly . . . so much for togetherness.

Creating our gingerbread house was an extravagantly messy affair. Not only because the pastry bag sprung a few leaks, but also because it was so hard to keep it twisted closed to keep the icing from squeezing out the wrong end! Eventually, we all used our hands to smear the royal icing "mortar" on the gingerbread pieces. The house wasn't much to begin with, but that didn't bother my sons. It worked well for target practice. It was decimated nearly as soon as it was built. Throughout the rest of the holiday season, I found reminders of our gingerbread fiasco—icing crusted on various knobs, dials, switches, and faucets.

Because I played the Christmas music in the DVD player, which was attached to the TV, Griffin couldn't understand why there was sound, but no picture. "Show?" he would ask plaintively, as he handed me the fingerprint-covered CD he'd just divested from the DVD player.

The only Christmas music we heard was when we were serenaded by Mark and Daniel belting out, "Jingle bells, Batman smells, the Joker learned ballet . . . hee-hee-hee, snicker, snicker, snort!"

They fought over the Advent calendar. Griffin's participation was limited to examining and then discarding the felt-and-Velcro nativity scene characters, much to the chagrin of his two rules-based, school-aged brothers, who tried in vain to keep the characters in sequential order beginning with the star, angel, and shepherds and ending with the Wise Men, gifts, and Jesus. Thinking I had found a solution, I moved the calendar to a less obvious spot. Unfortunately, we never ticked off another day.

The nativity set was reduced to a battle scene and the boys launched Baby Jesus off the roof of the crèche. That we still had tiny Baby Jesus and his little straw bed after four seasons was, in itself, one of the miracles of Christmas. Compounding their irreverence was the extent of their interest in our Advent celebration. The boys argued not only about who got to light the candles, but also who got to blow them out. Sometimes we lit them and blew them out repeatedly until everyone had an equal number of turns.

I was on overload, as I was essentially trying to cram five days worth of work into four days on top of all the added holiday hoopla, which resulted in my sampling *far* too many cookies and chocolates and drinking *way* too much coffee.

"It's chaos at my house," I concluded to Kathy.

She chuckled and nudged me. "C'mon, that's part of the fun!"

I rolled my eyes. "Uh-huh."

As I drove off that morning, I thought about our conversation. I really didn't want to be such a grinch, and Kathy was right—this was Christmas—all of the boys' antics should be taken in stride, because it really was part of the fun. Right then and there, I decided to embrace the pandemonium.

The rest of the holiday season included Griffin's new tradition of pulling pinecones, bells, and candy canes off the tree (the only things left on the bottom half) and hiding them around the house and Mark and Daniel's regular habit of shrieking potty words and scrapping like a couple of puppies. I knew that reminders of Santa Claus seeing them when they were sleeping, knowing when they were awake, and knowing if they'd been bad or good would be useless. I simply told them that I expected the mess to be cleaned up before they watched their superhero cartoons.

My children's gift to me was to remind me to view Christmas as they do. Once I aligned my vision with reality, I was fully able to enjoy the season. And pinecones, bells, and candy canes continued to surface until Easter.

Boy to the world!

Getting Christmas

BY SHAUNA SMITH DUTY

After circling the parking lot like a hungry buzzard, I finally spotted an empty space. I eased my car into a parking spot across from the toy store and looked at my daughter, Alysen, who sat bright eyed and anxious in the passenger seat.

"Well, let's do this thing," I said begrudgingly.

I didn't want to be out and about the day after Christmas looking for a rain check, even it was for a doll Alysen had waited for all year. This was my mother's doing. She had bestowed the honor of owning a coveted Doll of All Dolls onto her only granddaughter, and at the same time subjected me to one of the pitfalls of motherhood: guilt. When I suggested she order the doll online, I received a lecture about spending quality time with my daughter, which included a few potent words regarding the evils of Internet shopping as well. Rather than listen to me, she had accepted a rain check redeemable on the worst shopping day of the year—the day after Christmas—and from the busiest toy store in town!

How would my weathering the December 26 shopping madness at the crack of dawn make me a good mother? Did Alysen's dreams really consist of an eighteen-inch plastic doll with unblinking eyes and outfits that cost $40 a pop? I hoped not.

I locked the car and grabbed my daughter's mitten-covered hand. It wasn't as small as it used to be. Her fingers wrapped around my hand instead of nestling in my palm. Looking down at her, I realized she had grown. The top of her head now reached my shoulder. Soon, shopping for dolls would end and we'd be shopping for training bras and mini-skirts. Maybe Mother was right about the quality-time thing.

I pushed open the front door and stared at the throngs of people swarming the aisles like ants on spilled Kool-Aid. My head began to ache.

"There's Customer Service, Mom," Alysen said, pointing toward a line of shoppers. I groaned aloud and caught the timid smile that crossed her lips. "Thanks for bringing me?"

Reminding myself Alysen was only ten, I nodded and suppressed another groan. "You're welcome, Baby. Let's get in line."

After a few moments, Alysen pointed to a huge box. "What's that?" she asked.

"Looks like the toy drive." I glanced at my watch again.

"For the kids without families?"

I nodded impatiently. "It's a donation box to collect toys for orphans."

"You think Santa visited everybody? Even the orphans?" She pulled both of her lips between her teeth to conceal her smile.

"I'm pretty sure he did," I replied, trying to ignore the smirk on her face. I knew she wanted me to think she still believed in Santa—I actually liked the farce. As far as I was concerned, the longer she wanted me to view her as a baby, the better.

"Can I go read the sign on the box?"

We were both getting bored, and the line was stagnant. "Sure," I replied.

Suddenly, another cash register opened and, by some miracle, I was summoned to the front of the line. "Come on, Honey," I called to my daughter as I handed our rain check to the cashier. Within seconds, the cashier was shouting an item number over the crackling intercom. A few minutes later, a man showed up and handed the clerk a box. The cashier bagged it and lifted it over the counter.

I presented the bag to my daughter, who looked like I was offering her the Hope Diamond. *All of her dreams in a cardboard box. How simple.* After scribbling my signature on the receipt, I reached to grab my daughter's hand, but she was already at the doors. I smiled. *A crowd hater just like her ma.*

At the door, she slipped her hand in mine. "Mom, you deserve Starbucks."

I grinned. *All of my dreams in a paper cup? How simple.* "So do you, Sweetheart."

We ordered our favorite overpriced holiday beverages at the drive-through. Christmas was over. Life was grand. The lingering scent of coffee and peppermint filled the car as we headed for home. Pulling into the driveway, I parked the car and jumped out, slamming the door behind me. Like all experienced moms, my subconscious took inventory of my daughter's belongings as I stuck the key in the front door lock. She'd finished her cocoa in the car and had her coat, mittens, scarf, and . . . .

"Where's your bag?"

"Uh . . . " She shuffled her feet.

With a look of pure shock, I practically shouted, "No! Please tell me you didn't leave it at the store." Alysen's eyes welled with tears.

Pulling the key from the door handle, I took a deep breath and tried not to get angry. "It's okay, we'll go back. Just get in the car," I said. Alysen didn't move. "Come on, it's okay. Accidents happen."

"Oh, Mommy!" she wailed. In the next instant, she had buried her head in the front of my coat and wrapped her arms around my waist, nearly spilling my coffee.

I set my cup on the car and returned her hug, then pulled her from me and looked at her face. Tears streamed down her cheeks.

"What is it, Baby?"

She shook her head and sniffed a few times. "Don't be mad. Please don't be mad."

"I'm not mad." I wiped her tears with my thumbs.

She cocked her head and bit her lip. It took her a moment to speak. "I put it in the box."

"What?"

"The Toys for Orphans box. The sign said they would make their last pick up on December 26 at 9:00 A.M. Don't be mad." She gulped in a deep breath and started talking quickly, "But if Santa forgot *anybody*, and they don't have grandmas and moms and dads to give them stuff . . . then some kids may have gotten nothing." A new flood of tears splashed down her cheeks and she wailed, "And I already have so much."

I was speechless. She had given away her box of Christmas dreams come true—the Doll of All Dolls that she waited all year for—to the orphans? My heart was filled with admiration. My ten-year-old daughter had chosen self-sacrifice over her own desire.

"I'm not mad," I whispered, tears beginning to trickle down my face. "I'm so proud of you. You know what the Spirit of Christmas is."

Alysen wiped my tears with the back of one mitten and then sniffed, wiping at her own face. "I love Christmas," she said with a little shrug.

I smiled and pulled her into my arms, "I do, too, Baby. I do, too."

Safely Home

BY DELBERT L. BIEBER

In the predawn hours of Christmas Eve, we loaded the old Dodge panel truck with eggs, fresh chicken, winter turnips, potatoes, and an assortment of homemade baked goods and pies. By first light, we were on our way to the city.

It was exciting for a six-year-old boy to accompany his dad making door-to-door deliveries of the farm's produce. And to make it even more dreamlike, somewhere about mid-morning, snowflakes began to descend like little angels. Standing on the city sidewalk, I looked up at the dark gray sky to watch the snow falling softly, playfully.

"We must hurry now," Dad said with urgency in his voice and concern etched in his face.

Dad sent me on ahead to get the order from the next house, always keeping me one house ahead of him as we worked our way up one street and down the next. It was a great big step in parental trust and childhood responsibility, and I was feeling quite privileged. And of course, the fuss the housewives made of this "grown-up" little boy caused me to try even harder to do everything "just like Dad."

We were moving so fast and concentrating so hard, I barely noticed that the snow was continuing to mount, not only on the lawns and trees, but also on the sidewalks and streets. And by mid-afternoon, those soft, fluffy, drifting, angelic flakes had turned into biting, swirling, driven, demonic crystals. This was not just a friendly winter snow shower; it was a blizzard! By the time we finished the route in early evening, there was over twelve inches of snow on the ground, and more coming down. It was going to be a white Christmas indeed!

Between the city of Allentown and the tiny village of Old Zionsville, there are several treacherous mountains. That night, they were worse than treacherous; they were nearly impossible to negotiate. There were no tracks to follow in the freshly fallen snow. No snowplow had been over these mountains since the storm began; no one had, except my Dad and me.

The chains Dad had put on the truck tires before we left the city helped, but barely, and one of them had broken a link. With every revolution of the rear wheel, there was a clank against the fender. Several times, we stopped and Dad lifted me onto the hood to clear the snow from the windshield so he could see. But mostly, he just stuck his head out the side of the open door on the driver's side.

Finally, we arrived at the entrance to the lane that led to our farm house. Unfortunately, it was completely blocked with over three feet of snow. Consequently, Dad decided to attempt to drive across the windswept fields. For the next several hours, he drove about ten feet, got out of the truck, shoveled a bit, repaired the chains, got back into the truck, and drove about ten feet . . . and so it went. Though I was frightened, it didn't dampen my enthusiasm. I was glad I was there with Dad and he wasn't forced to deal with this storm on his own.

Somewhere near midnight, Dad realized driving was a hopeless cause. We loaded our arms with the most expensive perishable items and began to wade through the snow, toward what I hoped was home. The storm was furious. Ice crystals burned our faces and the ferocity of the wind took our breath away.

Less than five yards from the truck, Dad's flashlight died. The night was darker than black, and I hoped Dad knew where he was going. It was impossible to see anything in any direction. I stepped into his footsteps as he dragged his feet to make the path as easy as possible for me. Occasionally, he stopped to make sure I was all right. Several times I fell, and no sooner had I landed face first in the snow, than Dad's hands were there to pick me up again.

Then, just when I felt I couldn't take another step, Dad laid down his armful of produce to pick up a more valuable bundle: his shivering, fatigued little boy. For the remainder of the journey I rode home in the arms of my father. And when I saw the lights on the Christmas tree in the front window of our house, a wonderful sensation rejuvenated my entire being and I laughed as I hugged my dad. He had brought us safely home!

For Dad it was probably one of the worst days and nights of his life, but in my young mind, it had been a wonderful Christmas—I had been there to help Dad through a situation that could have been very frightening if he had had to deal with it on his own.

All I Want for Christmas

BY MARIE (NIKKI) ESSELSTEIN

It was Christmas Eve at the local department store. I stood in line and watched as the screaming boy in front of me was placed on Santa's lap. I clutched my mother's hand a little tighter, and trembled in my winter boots as I watched.

Santa was downright scary.

The little boy wriggled and fought to get away, but Santa had an iron grip. *Just let him go*, I begged silently. Instead, Santa held on until the boy calmed down.

"One, two, three," the too-tall elf said, and a flashbulb lit up the room.

Before Santa could ask the child what he wanted for Christmas, the little boy had slid down his leg and raced to the safety of his mother's arms. The boy clung to her, tears rolling down his face.

"Mommy," I whispered in abject horror, "he didn't tell Santa what he wanted!"

My mother smiled and patted me on the head. "That's alright, Sweetie. Santa has magic. He knows what every little girl and boy wants for Christmas."

I glanced up at her confident smile, then back at the little boy. *If Santa had magic, why hadn't he known the boy didn't want his picture taken?* I frowned, scrutinizing Santa one last time before I took a deep breath and moved toward him.

With each step, I visualized what I wanted for Christmas. Repeating to myself, *paint set, paint set, paint set,* I walked slowly, not stopping until I was directly in front of him. Santa looked down at me for a second, then put his big hands under my arms and lifted me to his lap. I barely breathed.

"Look here," the too-tall elf called. Santa and I turned toward the elf. "One, two, three!" Flash! The Polaroid spit out our image.

"So, what's your name?" Santa asked.

"Nikki," I answered, my brows puckering. An icicle of fear started at the base of my neck. *Didn't Santa recognize me?*

"And have you been good?"

I swallowed anxiously, the fear beginning to spread. Wasn't Santa supposed to know if I'd been good or not? Unable to speak, I nodded, fighting the urge to pull on his beard.

"So," he said, in a voice that had unexpectedly grown serious, "what do you want for Christmas?"

My eyes locked on his and I froze. *What was it I had wanted?* I couldn't remember. All I knew was that I wanted out of there and quick. Santa waited patiently. He looked over his half-moon glasses, blue eyes twinkling. I sat, completely numb, waiting for him to put me down so I could run to my mother, too.

Finally, he smiled. "How about a doll? Would you like a doll?"

I nodded feebly.

"I bet you'd like a Sleepy Sally doll," he suggested. "She closes her eyes when you lay her down and wets when you feed her. Would you like that?"

I nodded again, my eyes darting around the room in search of my mother. When I found her, she was smiling.

"Well, that sounds good to me!" Santa replied with a jolly laugh. Then he gave me a squeeze and set my feet back on the floor. I walked to my mother on wobbly legs and watched, impressed, as the next child—a boy who was at least seven, and therefore much braver than me—practically jumped into Santa's lap.

We walked out of the fake snow-covered kingdom and right into the toy department. Near the exit was a huge well-stocked pile of Sleepy Sally dolls in their signature pink boxes. I took one look at the dolls and realized what I had done.

I had ruined my only chance of ever getting the one thing I so desperately wanted. Overwhelmed, I began to cry. All I wanted for Christmas was a paint set from the hobby store where Daddy got the toy train parts for my brother. The paint set with the four big jars of beautiful blue, green, yellow, and red. The paint set that came with eight wonderful brushes. The paint set with the mixing tray and the water bowl included.

But it was too late. I looked across the room at the line of children still waiting to see Santa. I knew my mother would never let me wait in that line a second time. I looked at the pile of Sleepy Sallies and wiped my face on my sleeve, resigned to my sad fate.

It took forever to get to sleep on Christmas Eve. When I finally did sleep, my dreams were filled with visions of paint sets and dolls. My brother woke me twice during the night—both times, he was sure he'd heard reindeer hooves on the roof.

I was the last to wake the next morning. Reluctantly, I made my way into the living room. My brother had gotten tons of new Hot Wheels, just what he had asked for. I didn't want to look under the tree—I knew what waited there. But as I walked into the living room, I glanced toward the tree anyway. I didn't see anything pink. Instead, I saw an easel with a big pad of paper on it, and right in front of it was a paint set! The perfect paint set!

I sprinted into the room and grabbed the paint set. I could hardly believe my eyes!

"Mommy! Daddy!" I shouted, racing into the kitchen where they were talking. "I thought he was going to bring me that Sleepy Sally doll but he brought me the paint set!"

I looked from Dad's wide smile to Mom's confident, perfect smile, and that's when it all clicked. Mom wore the same smile she had shot across the room to me that day in Santaland. The same smile that had been on her face when she told me Santa was magical and that he knew everything.

Standing there in the kitchen—in my pajamas and bare feet, staring at my mother's confident smile—was a defining moment for me that I will never forget. That's when it all clicked for me, and I knew.

Santa really did have magic and really did know everything. Why did I suddenly believe it was true? Not because Santa had brought me the paint set, but because Mom had said he would. When Mom told me Santa had magic and that he knew everything, I should have believed her. For that one brief moment, I had forgotten that Mom, of all people, would know! She had proven to me time and time again that she had more magic than anyone.

Mother Knows Best

by Sharon Sheppard

G rowing up in a small, northern Minnesota village had lots of advantages, but shopping wasn't one of them. Long before the Mall of America was even a gleam in some greedy developer's eye—before anyone had ever heard of iPods or designer jeans, even in the city—our little community could just as well have been located in the tundra of the Northwest Territories for all the conveniences it offered.

We lived in God's Country, we bragged, as though that could make up for our backward isolation, but scenery provided scant comfort when the holidays rolled around. Because the block-long Main Street offered few options, our Christmas shopping was limited to Cofflands' Hardware, Reynolds' Dry Goods Store, or the Sears catalog.

The long-anticipated Christmas catalog arrived in late October, and it was wondrous to behold. My three brothers and I fought for turns. We pored over the toy section until the catalog was dog-eared. Our wants changed daily, as we daydreamed about how each item would make our lives richer. My brothers coveted sleds, jackknives, baseballs, and board games, while I focused on tin tea sets and paper dolls.

We made copious lists—complete with page numbers and catalog numbers—for our parents' convenience. We ranked and prioritized our choices, fantasizing about what we would really like to have if money were no object. But, of course, money was always an object. Even at a tender age, we were aware that money dictated how elaborate our holiday would or would not be. With that in mind, we narrowed our lists to a few favorites among the items we figured might fall within the realm of financial possibility.

To help visualize the actual size of each item, we used a ruler. But even though we now had an idea of the size, would the toy look as good in person as it did in the catalog? We could never be sure.

According to our parents, we had to make sure we knew which toy we wanted well in advance. The catalog order had to be sent in at least three weeks before Christmas to ensure delivery on time. Even if the order was sent in on time, it wasn't unheard of for Sears to send a partial order with several items on the invoice marked, "SORRY, NOT AVAILABLE." That meant starting all over again or settling for something from the inventory at Cofflands' or Reynolds'.

The Christmas I was six years old, I yearned for a doll. I drooled over the choices in the catalog for days, contrasting the large expensive dolls with real hair and elegant wardrobes with baby dolls that had eyes that opened and closed. The biggest dolls were definitely out of our price range, but maybe my mother, who was an excellent seamstress, could sew some doll clothes for one of the smaller ones, I reasoned.

Christmas neared, and even though I figured the Sears order had already been mailed in—maybe even delivered and hidden under our parents' bed—my tastes still fluctuated from day to day. Right up until the holidays, I kept changing my mind.

A couple of days before Christmas, I sat at the kitchen table with the catalog, now virtually in shreds from wear, and watched as my mother punched down the bread dough.

"See any dolls you like?" she asked.

I scanned my favorite page, then said, "I like 'em all. All except this one." I pointed to a nondescript baby doll with light brown molded hair and not much of a wardrobe.

A strange look flickered across my mother's face. "What don't you like about that one?" she asked.

"I don't know. I just don't like it," I replied. "Maybe I'm getting too old for baby dolls."

As I examined the catalog page again, wondering which baby doll was my absolute favorite, Mom covered the pan of bread with a dishtowel and went about her chores quietly.

On Christmas Eve, the house nearly burst with excitement. I couldn't wait to open my gifts!

After supper, we sang "Silent Night," and my brothers and I performed the recitations we had memorized for the church program. Then our father read the Christmas story from Luke 2, and he prayed for the *longest* time. He thanked God for all our blessings—naming them one by one—while we fidgeted, knowing we should be more interested in the *real* meaning of Christmas, but wishing we could get on with our gifts all the same.

I just knew the rectangular box with my name on it was going to hold the doll of my dreams. Would it be the one with the sailor dress and patent leather shoes? Or had my mother chosen the kewpie doll in the yellow dress with a smocked yoke? They were both beauties and I knew I would love either of them dearly. Finally, the box was in my lap, and though I tried not to tear the paper so we could use it again next year, suddenly I couldn't wait a moment longer.

When I had ripped off the paper and removed the lid, my eyes grew wide and my bottom lip quivered. There, nestled in the box—wrapped in a fluffy, blue flannel blanket was the very baby doll I had told my mother I did not like, the plain doll with the molded brown hair. Stunned, all I could do was stare at her in surprise. The doll was dressed in a miniature nightcap and a tiny baby bottle was tucked into the box. I slipped my hand into the blanket and uncovered the doll. Under her wrap, she wore a soft pink gown and a real diaper.

I gazed at the doll for a long time. Then I rubbed the soft downy flannel between my fingers. Hesitantly, my fingers touched her soft body. Before I knew it, I had untied her nightcap. As gently as I could, I ran my hands over her molded head and smiled. The whole while, she looked back at me with big blue eyes. She seemed different from the catalog picture, and bigger than the ruler measure had indicated so many weeks ago.

The longer I studied her, the more wonderful she looked. She was not at all boring like her catalog picture indicated. As I stared at her, I suddenly felt as if we belonged together. In the blink of an eye, a new question surfaced: Is this the way real mothers looked at their newborns for the first time?

Later that night, I took the doll to bed with me and hugged her tightly. She was soft and cuddly. My mind wandered back to the days of sitting in front of the catalog and making my decisions. I had felt I was old enough for a more grown-up doll, but I was sure thankful not to have to try to snuggle up to some stiff-haired thing with patent leather shoes. Besides, I thought as I nestled beneath the blankets with my soft doll, babies are what Christmas is all about in the first place.

Evergreen

BY LESLIE J. WYATT

Most Christmas presents are wrapped in paper and tied with ribbons. They come, they go, as is the way with all material things. But there is another kind of gift—ever fresh and evergreen—that cannot be touched or placed beneath a tree. It is one of the latter sort of gifts that comes to mind when I recall a certain childhood Christmas.

I was almost six that year. In my eyes, we had the most beautiful tree and the largest pile of presents in the whole universe. But one element that charged this day, with a particular magic, was Daddy. He was home, and everything felt so right, so perfect.

Daddy drove a long-haul truck in those days. He traversed the nation two weeks at a time, and every time he drove that big rig out of the driveway, a lifetime seemed to pass before he returned.

He had twinkling blue eyes and close-cropped black curls. In his own quiet way, he could handle any emergency—from flat tires to frozen water pipes—as easily as he could hop on one foot. He was my hero and my safety all wrapped up together, and I loved him desperately. So, for him to be home, sitting in our tiny living room that Christmas—sipping coffee and chatting with Mama—was as if God was smiling in heaven and not one thing was amiss in all of creation.

I had spent Daddy's last absence wondering what amazing gift he would bring me. Surely he would have come across the most perfect, the most exciting item a six year old could ever want. I envisioned a new doll: It would be so lifelike, so soft of skin and sweet of face, it would rival my new baby sister!

But if he hadn't found that kind of doll, maybe he had found the kitchen of my little girl dreams. When I closed my eyes, I clearly envisioned him stowing my kitchen on top of his load and heading homeward. It would have a real sink that would hold water and have cupboard shelves with real food. And a Magic-Bake Oven that I could use to turn out chocolate chip cookies like Mama made.

Those were the two things I wanted the most. At first glimpse into the living room that Christmas morning, I saw neither. But there were so many other packages, such laughter, such excitement, that I hardly gave it a thought. Secure in the conviction that there must be something even more wonderful than a baby doll or a real kitchen, I gave myself to the delicious process of ripping paper, thankful hugs, and myriad new possessions.

About halfway through the pile, there it was: *To Leslie, from Daddy.* The smallness of the package took me by surprise. It was barely eight inches tall and half that wide. But I flashed Daddy my very biggest smile so he would know how much I loved him as I tore at the wrapping paper.

The first thing I saw was a goofy-looking plastic clown face with a bulbous nose, rolling eyes, and a tongue lolling out one corner of its painted mouth. Pulling off the remainder of the paper, I discovered scarlet fur and two red-felt feet of overwhelming proportions.

I gulped. Part of me had known I shouldn't hope for expensive things like dolls or kitchens, but this was so far removed from anything I'd expected. . . .

I petted the fur carefully. "What is it, Daddy?" I asked, hoping he couldn't read the utter disappointment clogging my throat and burning in my eyes.

He shrugged. "A playtoy?" Then he laughed, and I did my best to laugh as well.

When a younger sister claimed my attention, I laid Daddy's gift aside, turning back to the shrinking pile of presents.

The day was long, as Christmas days tend to be, with the arrival of grandparents, a big meal, and new possessions. When Daddy said his farewells, climbed into his truck, and drove off to deliver his waiting load, I was deep into a game of Ka-Boom! Before I realized exactly what was happening, his taillights had flashed a final goodbye.

I don't remember much of the rest of the evening, but later—when the house was quiet and dark—I lay on my bed reliving the day, and my six-year-old heart ached. Daddy was gone, and what if he knew I didn't like the playtoy? *Would he think I didn't love him? Was he crying in his truck right now, all by himself?* The pain of it pressed down on me with such weight that I finally dragged myself out of bed and trailed through the quiet house to the kitchen, tears running down my cheeks.

Lost in my misery, I didn't notice my mother sitting in her white wooden rocker. But she saw me. With gentle hands, she drew me into her lap and let me sob against her shoulder.

"What's wrong, honey?"

Too sad and ashamed to tell her, I whispered, "I don't know." And then I cried some more, for the lie I had told.

"Everything seems harder when you're tired," she said. "Just go to sleep, and things will be brighter in the morning."

Her hand was soft on my hair, the house quiet around us. Surrounded by her love, filled with love for her and for the daddy who had cared enough about me to give me a present, even if it wasn't a doll or a kitchen, the ache within began to ease. I let the old, familiar creaking of the rocking chair lull me to sleep.

Many Christmases have come and gone since then. The furry red playtoy has gone the way of all toys. But the gift my mother gave me there in her old white rocker—her gentle love wrapped in wise words and comforting arms—that gift lives as fresh and evergreen in my heart as if it were given just last night.

A Good Song for Shaving

BY FRANCES HILL ROBERTS

In 1945, I woke to the predawn darkness of my eighth Christmas and decided this was the day I would ask. As though the boldness of my thought had disturbed their sleep, my sisters, Sarah and Beth, turned in perfect unison to face opposite walls, pulling the blanket taut and sending a draft across my bird-slip shoulders. I burrowed deeper under the covers between them and wondered if they were dreaming of fat red men pushing glittery toys down sooty chimneys.

Magic, for me, lay closer to home—in hands calloused from caring, in a voice that bellowed us to supper by a slanted sun on short winter days—in the sounds of snoring, drifting down spooky hallways, assuring me that all was well. In the comfort of my bed, I wiggled in anticipation: This was the day I would ask.

When I woke a second time, it was to the aroma of fresh-brewed coffee. Mama was awake. Leaving the warmth of my blanketed womb, I crawled to the foot of the bed and stepped onto the icy linoleum. My feet flew down the freezing stairs to the warmth of the kitchen with the speed of hummingbirds' wings. There, I climbed into a chair to watch my parents' morning rituals.

My mother frowned. "What are you doing up so early?"

"I couldn't sleep," I said, praying she would let me stay.

Mama nodded in understanding, then smiled. "Well, as long as you don't get underfoot, you can stay." Walking to the foot of the stairs, she called, "Tom! Water's heating."

My father walked in, smelling of yesterday's undershirt and wood shavings caught in the cuffs of his trousers. A superstitious man, he thought it bad luck to bathe at night, so he woke each morning littered with labor from the day before. His hair was askew with cowlicks and dark stubble covered his face.

Just then, Sarah and Beth wandered into the room rubbing sleepiness from their eyes. "Did he come?" they asked.

"This is all he left," my father said with a grin, reaching under the table and pulling out a bucket filled with coal for feeding the fire-breathing furnace in the cellar below.

"Hush, Tom," Mama said, a frown appearing on her unlined face. "You'll spoil their Christmas!" Glancing at her children, she smiled. "You can have your stockings while you eat breakfast," she said, as she unpinned the stockings from the windowsill.

The stockings were identical, for my father always wore black socks. The bulge in the toe was the size of an orange; the foot, lumpy with walnuts; the leg, apple shaped; and a peppermint candy cane peeked over the top. I peeled my orange in an ecstasy of anticipation, wondering what waited under the Christmas tree in the living room.

Decorating the tree was, to my father, what cooking was to my mother: artistry in motion. The ritual had begun two days before, when my father bartered poor Mr. Endsor down to half price for the finest tree on the lot. Daddy hauled the tree home in the Radio Flyer wagon we used to carry groceries.

"Have you lost your mind?" Mama cried when she saw the tree. "It's ten feet tall!"

"It's perfect!" proclaimed Daddy, prepared to abandon sanity entirely in service of the consummate Christmas tree.

After balancing the tree in a bucket of sand, he created an intricate latticework of string from the tree trunk to the wall. Once satisfied that no tree had ever stood so straight, he immersed himself in the core of his Christmas madness: the lights. Each strand was meticulously separated, every bulb tested. They were then arranged on the tree no less painstakingly than the painting of the Sistine Chapel. Daisy chains of hooks were untangled and shiny red and green balls strategically placed between silver stars and frosted angels. Finally, the tinsel was hung, carefully supervised by my father, who insisted clumping was a crime against the Spirit of Christmas everywhere.

At last, the tree was declared decorated, and we all stood back for the big moment. Even Mama came in from the kitchen to watch. Daddy picked up the plug and lit the tree. Its beauty took my breath away.

But now it was Christmas morning, and we'd finished the mandatory nibbles of breakfast. We tore down the hall to the living room. There she was, seated beside the plaster nativity scene, yellow-yarn hair flowing down her back, painted blue eyes, shiny black shoes—Sparkle Plenty, one of the two gifts we'd each been allowed to ask Santa for. Next to the doll sat *The Complete Tales of Uncle Wiggly*. Everything I'd asked for was there. Still, I longed for one thing more, something I'd been thinking about since the Christmas before, a question I had lacked the courage to ask until now.

I walked down the hall to the dining room. There he sat, cracking walnuts in his calloused hands, two at a time. I stood beside his chair, and felt anxiety flutter along the lining of my stomach like moth wings.

I took a deep breath. "Daddy, can I watch you shave?" He brushed walnut dust from his hands, as though he hadn't heard. I asked a second time. "Daddy, can I watch you shave?"

He glanced down at me. "Watch me shave?" Then he shrugged. "I guess so."

I was ecstatic. At last, I would get to see the morning ritual that transformed a bewhiskered carpenter into the handsome head of the house my mother had chosen to be our father. It seemed eons before my mother said, "Tom, you'd better get cleaned up for dinner."

When Daddy started toward the stairs, my castle collapsed. Then he turned to me and said, "Come on." Overflowing with joy, I followed him up the steps and down the hall. At the bathroom door, he swooped me up and plopped me on the clothes hamper. Running the water hot enough to cause steam, he wet a washcloth and held it against his face, softening the whiskers. Taking hold of the razor strop, he honed the blade to a fine, sharp edge. Setting it aside, he retrieved his shaving mug from the medicine cabinet and lathered his face. The clean smell of Old Spice drifted into my corner of the room, making me feel unaccountably secure while he scraped swatches of sled tracks through Christmas snow, down his face and up his neck.

At last, it began—the distant rumble I had waited for. Sternum swept from the floor of his lungs, full blown at the vocal cords, my father's voice burst forth in song as he paid tribute to his hero, John Henry, champion of laborers, who had died hammering spikes to build the American railroad. My heart danced in time to his lyrics. Never had there been a better song for shaving—never would there be a more cherished Christmas present!

Getting It Right

BY HELEN C. COLELLA

I grew up in Newark, New Jersey, and lived in a gigantic five-story apartment complex that encompassed an entire city block. Five well-groomed, meticulously maintained courtyards housed anywhere from eighty to one hundred and ten families, all of whom knew you, your family, and most of your business. Neighbors were friends and more—they cared about you.

The residents, as did the management, took pride in the complex.

Each season brandished its own strong points: lush green lawns, colorful flowerbeds, and blooming trees surrounded by paths that led from one courtyard to the other, providing a sanctuary in which to appreciate Mother Nature. Year-round family activities also flourished, allowing for working parents to enjoy special time with their children and friends.

Yet, despite all the amenities this mini village provided, it is Christmastime that stands out most in my memory. When I close my eyes and think about my childhood, the decorations that adorned the courtyards, the giant nativity scene in the playground, the evergreen tree with its festive lights, the children's gift exchange, and, of course, that visit from old St. Nick—and his candy cane treat for every child—are the first visions that come to mind. I can still hear the voices of the children strolling along, caroling to those who could not participate, but who cheered and clapped as we paraded along the courtyards. I still feel the closeness and love everyone so generously shared.

Christmas meant church, family gatherings, and enjoying the holiday season, all within personal parameters. None of the residents were wealthy, but some of the families splurged on real Christmas trees, which seemed like a very big deal to me. We were hardworking families, all trying to make ends meet to the best of our ability, and most of us owned artificial Christmas trees that could be used year after year.

For as long as I can remember, an artificial tree held the place of honor in our house. We simply couldn't afford to buy a new tree every year. Owning an artificial tree meant convenience for a busy mom with a full-time job. Mom had to go to the storage room, rummage through the boxes where our tree and decorations lived, and drag it all back up to our fifth-floor unit. My brother and I took it from there.

One of the artificial trees, a replica of a traditional six-foot Douglas fir, lasted several years. We dressed it up so well you could hardly tell it wasn't real. We decorated every single branch. However, somewhere in between the years of the Douglas fir's longevity, Mother surprised us with a few novelty trees, as well.

One year, an all-white tree joined the ranks of our holiday décor and overwhelmed everyone. It stands out stark and sterile in my mind. I remember my dumbfounded expression and the question that popped out before I could contain it.

"Did you bleach out the green six-footer?"

Mom had scowled in response. "It's the style for this year," she answered. "We're going to decorate it in red."

The following year we had a white-on-white treatment with the same tree.

"Classy," Mom exclaimed, pleased by the overall appearance. No one challenged her remark to her face, but when she turned around to admire her classy purchase, Dad shook his head.

"Don't worry, kids," he whispered, "she'll get it right one of these times."

Then it happened. The holiday season that hurled all of us into a state of shock. Mom came home with an enormous *silver foil* tree.

"We don't need any decorations at all this year," she informed us with an air of authority no one dared to question. Then, with the grace of a fashion model, she plugged in a multicolored, rotating-light mechanism. "Just watch." Her eyes twinkled as the lights changed colors from red to green to yellow to blue. The foil picked up and reflected each color handsomely.

"In effect," she added with a satisfied smile, "we have four different trees!"

We all nodded, unenthusiastically, and then waited patiently for the foil tree to be replaced by what we hoped would someday be the perfect Christmas tree.

As Dad had said, Mom would eventually get it right. I hadn't expected it would happen so quickly, or that it would come about because of a family tragedy, but I suppose all things happen for a reason, and perhaps the perfect tree was waiting to be there for us when we most needed it.

Our perfect Christmas tree appeared the year Dad died. Mom tried to keep the spirit of the season going strong for the family, and in her mind that meant finding the right Christmas tree. This task had always fallen on her shoulders, but this year she took the responsibility very seriously.

Her exact words had been, "I'll take care of it. Nothing too big. Nothing too fancy. Nothing but a tree."

With "artificial mode" still in mind, Mom busied herself in the living room putting the Christmas tree up. Before long, she had set up a small green tabletop model and adorned it with nothing but a silver star.

I recall the word that slipped through my mind when I walked into the room and looked at her newest creation: perfect. My eyes glistened with unshed tears. At long last, Mom had gotten it right. And I knew in my heart of hearts that Dad would have loved this tree.

An Aunt Sunne Christmas

BY LYNN RUTH MILLER

Aunt Sunne celebrated Christmas the way they do in storybooks. Her tree was like a page from a Victorian scrapbook—covered with tiny gingerbread men and hand-painted angels she had made when she was a child. She tucked antique wooden clowns and dancing elves between garlands of berries and strings of popcorn to create a tree so exquisite it sparkled with heavenly light. It became a tradition for our family to gather at her house on Christmas Day to celebrate and bond together after a year pursuing our own directions.

We had more fun at Aunt Sunne's house, with its overflow of books, music, dog bones, and playbills, than we could even imagine in a stadium or a movie theater. At Aunt Sunne's, we rekindled the lost art of conversation. We relaxed in those worn-out chairs of hers and exchanged one story after another about the neighbor who iced in his front porch when he tried to clear the snow from his drive or a clerk at the grocery store who couldn't count change. We told jokes on ourselves, and the more eggnog we drank, the harder we laughed.

The best part of the afternoon was when we opened the gifts my aunt had chosen for each of us. It was Aunt Sunne who gave me my first adult novel and tickets for a live stage production. It was she who gave me a Broadway musical record album and a doll as big as I was, to cuddle when I felt alone.

As the years went by, we separated to make lives of our own, but still, until the year Aunt Sunne turned eighty, we came together at her house on Christmas Day to experience family. That last year, I visited her the night before to help her put up the tree. That's when she told me she had sold the house and was moving into a small apartment.

"What do I need with such a big house now that I am alone?" she asked, and I was overwhelmed with a sense of loss.

Ignoring the lump in my throat, I asked, "Do you need help wrapping your gifts this year, Aunt Sunne?"

"Oh no!" she said. "This year I did my shopping on the telephone. I called Doubleday's and they sent all my selections wrapped and ready to give. See?" she said, pointing to a large pile of books with festive ribbons on them.

On Christmas day, we decided to save Sunne the trouble of cooking for so large a crowd. Sunne's brother, Bobby, and his wife Em, brought the turkey and the sweet potatoes, and my mother made a casserole and a pumpkin chiffon pie. I provided the eggnog and plum pudding. After dinner, we all gathered around that glorious tree for the last time, and Aunt Sunne handed each of us her offering.

"The lady at the store forgot to put in cards," she said, "but I can tell which present belongs to whom by its size."

Aunt Sunne's selections were always unusual, but this year, she really amazed us. My father received a book on twenty-four positions for a happier marriage; my mother's volume was entitled *How to Stalk Lions in Africa during Winter Months*. My sister's book discussed Hindu dietary habits, and Bobby, now a grandfather with lumbago, received a belly dancing manual. My book analyzed winning moves in Sumo wrestling, and Em, whose arthritis had crippled her fingers years ago, received an illustrated collection of piano melodies for jazz professionals.

When it was time to leave, we thanked Aunt Sunne for another perfect day and for the gifts she had given us. "Next year, we'll celebrate in my apartment," she said, but we knew no one-bedroom flat could hold the kind of Christmas we had returned to year after year. We would never again gather around a magic tree that emanated celestial light, or relive our family memories on her sagging, worn-out couch.

We stopped to chat outside on the street and my sister shook her head. "Aunt Sunne is really losing it, isn't she?" she said. "What ridiculous gifts she gave us! They had nothing to do with who we really are."

"So what?" I replied. "Her gifts tell us she loves each of us in a different way. Aunt Sunne's real Christmas present to us is her affirmation of our importance to each other. She has given a meaning to this holiday that we will carry in our hearts no matter where we are throughout the year. Now it's time for her to sit back and let us create our own 'Aunt Sunne Christmas.' All we have to do is remind one another that every individual has something unique to offer that enriches the world."

"Sure, Lynn Ruth," said my sister. "And will you be inviting us to your wrestling match next year?"

"Indeed I will," I said, "If you promise not to eat a cow and Em does a majestic piano roll to announce my entrance!"

Em giggled. "Count on me," she said. "And if your mother isn't killed by a lion or your father's practice moves, let's have it at my house next year. We'll let Sunne choose the tree!"

And that's what we did.

These days, every December 25th, I close my eyes and remember Aunt Sunne and, as if by magic, I am filled with wonder at the beauty of the season. Once again, I am warmed by that perfect tree of hers and the wonderfully comforting sense of family. And with that thought, this newest Christmas, the one we are about to celebrate, becomes another rare jewel in my box of precious Aunt Sunne memories.

Growing Up Cool

BY NANCY JO ECKERSON

My family was not wealthy when I was growing up. It was a beautiful life, although not lavish, by any means. Dad was a teacher and Mom was a housewife, so we often did without the frills and frivolous things in life. We counted on hand-me-downs from siblings for our wardrobes, and made good use of our imaginations for coming up with creative ways to play all day.

One standing rule in my house: In order to get new jackets, coats, mittens, or boots, you have to have totally outgrown your current attire. That was about the only excuse you could have. Holes in the clothes were patched, socks were darned, but if you just plain got too tall, then and only then, could you escape from that article of clothing.

It was the start of my thirteenth winter, and junior high school was even more daunting than I had imagined. The importance of looking right and acting cool could never be overstated for a seventh grader. The customary summer/winter clothing switch uncovered a very unfortunate fact—last winter's coat still fit perfectly. The current junior high fashion rage for those of us in the Buffalo area was to wear reversible ski jackets, and everybody who was anybody owned one—along with a membership in the local ski club.

By late November, I gave in and wore the "baby" coat from elementary school. My world didn't end, but I can't say it was a stellar time, either. Then, to add insult to injury, while Mom and I were Christmas shopping for relatives, I spied the most perfectly cool, quilted, red, reversible ski jacket at Hens and Kelly's department store. Mom watched as I tried it on and spun left and right in the mirror admiring myself. I did look really good in that red jacket. The reverse side was a pink and red floral print on a white background. I was beaming as I wrapped myself up in the pink hues of this exquisite find.

I gave Mom my best pitch, but of course, I knew: I didn't need the jacket.

Honestly, I was amazed at how I took the news. Maybe I was maturing, because I didn't even pout, and like most seventh-grade girls, I had pouting down to a fine art. But, I really understood that year that my parents were doing their best for me, so I let it go.

Nonetheless, Christmas morning brought excitement, as always. I had to admit, even opening our stockings was still entertaining, in a "reminds me of when I was little" kind of way. The sweet fragrance of oranges tucked in the toe of the stocking wafted throughout my bedroom.

At the end of the morning, I didn't even get as many presents as my big brother, JD, but I was fine. This was the first year I was able to work—cleaning houses and babysitting—enough hours to save a tidy sum to buy gifts. Most of my energy that morning went into watching my family members as they opened the presents I had bought them.

So, that was the first Christmas of my mature life. I was cool, and content to be cool.

All the gifts were unwrapped and a collective sigh of delirious exhaustion washed over us all. Mom had gone to turn on the oven for the Christmas turkey and little brother Steve was busy with a racing car. Suddenly, Mom appeared in the doorway with one more box. She said she had found it on the way to the kitchen and that it had my name on it.

Forsaking my teenage cool image, I leapt into the air and grabbed the box. Whew! It was a fair Christmas after all. Just having the same number of gifts was enough, but when I opened that box, my whole mindset concerning grace changed. There, tucked between layers of crisp white tissue, was the most gorgeous red, reversible ski jacket, with pink floral print on the reverse side. I knew the sacrifice my mother made to get me this jacket. I knew the customary rules that had to be broken, too. My mom was now elevated to a complete hippie—totally cool in my book. Thanks to my very loving mom, my teenage years were off to a great start.

The Christmas Gifts

BY RAYMOND L. ATKINS

Financially, it had been a tough year for our family. With Christmas coming, my wife, Marsha, and I were nearing wit's end about how we were going to purchase gifts for our four children. Because of some disappointing Christmases we had experienced as children, it had become important to us to provide a big Christmas for our kids. This year, however, we were going to have to lower our sights. I'd been sick and money was tight. It looked like this was going to be a Christmas of winter coats, socks, and underwear—basic necessities only. There just wasn't any way around it.

The three younger children were at the ages where a few dollars worth of brightly colored plastic went a long way, and they were still about as likely to play with the boxes as with the toys. It did not take much to make them happy, which was a good thing, because "not much" was exactly what was heading their way.

But our eldest child, Natalie, wanted a computer, and not just any computer. Unfortunately, for us, she had set her sights high. She wanted a better computer than NASA had owned when they put two men on the moon! She wanted a computer that would draw and design—one that would navigate the Internet *and* compose music. She wanted a computer that would write, print, edit, walk, talk, and shave. She wanted the super-duper deluxe model that could do just about anything except pay for itself.

"What are we going to do?" I asked Marsha late one night. It was about a week before Christmas, and I was all out of ideas. I jokingly added that since I didn't own a gun or a ski mask, robbing a store was out of the question. I had all but pulled up the floorboards in the old part of the house in search of Confederate gold. It was just no use. My pockets remained empty.

Marsha looked at me with luminous eyes and a confident tone. "We're going to get her what we can afford, tell her that we love her, and wish her a Merry Christmas," she explained. "And that will be that!" She paused and touched my shoulder gently. "She knows you've been sick and that things have been tough around here. She will just have to understand."

Did I mention that the woman I married is a genius? The thought of telling the truth never entered my mind.

That afternoon, we sat down with our nine-year-old daughter and explained the financial facts of life. We told her we loved her and that a computer was definitely in her future at some point, but for now, we just couldn't manage it. Then we asked her if there was something else she might like, something a little closer to the reality of our budget. By way of a reply, she asked if she could think about it for a while. We told her that would be fine. Then, as if we hadn't just destroyed her hopes of a good Christmas, which we most definitely had, she got up from her chair and went off to do her homework.

"Well, that wasn't so bad," my wife noted.

"I'll be laying on the railroad tracks if you need me," I replied, totally exhausted from the whole ordeal.

The rest of the day passed without incident, but by bedtime, Natalie still had not gotten back to us about her replacement gift and I began to get nervous.

"Don't worry about it," Marsha said before we went to sleep that night. "She's just disappointed. If she doesn't tell us something in a day or two, we'll ask her again."

The following day, I found the note.

The kids were at school, Marsha was at work, and I was straightening the house when I noticed a slip of paper sticking out of Natalie's Christmas stocking. I took the note to the kitchen table, smoothed it out, and read the following words:

Dear Santa and Jesus,

My dad has been sick and he can't buy me a computer. But that's ok. Can you bring me a puppy instead? If you bring me a puppy, then my Mom and Dad won't have to spend any money. And can you please make my Dad better, too?

Merry Christmas and I love you.

That evening I showed the note to my wife. We looked at each other, unable to speak. Finally, she broke the silence.

"Santa *and* Jesus," she said, shaking her head. "Talk about hauling out the big guns."

I nodded, proud of my young daughter. She was giving up a lot to make sure things worked out for her parents.

"If you get the dog," I said sheepishly, "I'll take care of getting better." Marsha nodded and squeezed my hand. We both knew noncompliance with this particular note was not an option. A canine would be joining our family.

It turned out to be a wonderful Christmas for all of us. The little ones got a few trucks and dolls, socks and underwear, and enjoyed playing with the boxes and wrappings a great deal. Our eldest—much wiser than her nine years let on—got Baby, a cocker spaniel whose first home had been a Dumpster. Marsha got a bottle of rank perfume and an armload of child-made treasures. And I got two presents: I got my health back, for which I thank both Santa and Jesus, *and* I got a reminder that the best gifts are the ones that money can't buy.

Time of Delight

BY VIVIENNE MACKIE

"Shh!" Denise whispered. "Mom will come!"

But as our blanket tent collapsed on top of the three of us, even Denise dissolved into another bout of giggling.

I was the only one who noticed the bedroom door open, as Mom peered in, then closed it again quietly. She knew what was going on, but realized it was a special time for us three girls, a special time that was repeated each year at Christmas.

Many people don't have good or treasured memories of Christmas and the holiday season, so I feel very lucky. I know from experience that good memories are not linked to money or how many presents you get for Christmas. Rather, good memories come from having family and special friends close by, and from creating a tradition or ritual that binds people together and makes them feel part of a select group.

Our tradition revolved around Turkish Delight.

Even though our family had little money to spare when I was growing up in Rhodesia (now Zimbabwe), we always loved Christmas. Christmas was when my Gran and Grandad drove their little car—loaded down with mysterious packets and a basket of yummy goodies—all the way from Umtali, a town about sixty miles away, to stay with us.

They slept in my small bedroom, which I didn't have to share, like my sisters did. So, while they visited, I slept with two of my four sisters, Denise and Veronita, who were just younger than me. We slept head to toe, with my pillow at the end of the bed, and strangely, we did sleep—a bit.

It was a time of intense anticipation and excitement, a buildup to the big day, so late at night we'd still be whispering together. And, quite by accident, a special sister ritual developed between us that included Turkish Delight.

Only at Christmas did Mom and Dad buy the sweet candy called Turkish Delight. Because it was so scarce, it became a symbol of the season to us. A week before Gran and Grandad arrived, we all went to Mrs. Simpson's general shop in the village, hoping and praying that the Turkish Delight had already arrived. It had! We were lucky that Mrs. Simpson put in a special order to a big shop in the capital of Salisbury, because many people in our small town wanted the delicacy, too! We gazed at the big open box on the counter with layers of Turkish Delight nestled on soft pink-and-white tissue paper and our mouths watered. Pink-and-white paper for the pink-and-white sweet seemed totally appropriate to us. One year, there had been green tissue too, which we later discovered was for the pistachio-flavored Delight. Powdered sugar coated each of the pieces, which were cut into neat blocks about one inch square.

The number of pieces we purchased depended on how much money Mom and Dad had saved throughout the year, and that number was always divisible by nine. That way Gran, Grandad, Mom, Dad, me, and all four of my sisters would have the same number of pieces.

"I think we saved three pounds this year," Mom said to Dad. "Hmm, then we can buy about seventy-five pieces?"

"Vee," Dad called, "come and do the sum. We need a number divided by nine so everyone gets the same."

At nine years old, I was able to decipher the figure quickly. "I think seventy-two is the closest," I said, my fingers and mind calculating as fast as I could. "So . . . we all get . . . um . . . eight pieces!"

Mrs. Simpson allowed us girls to help put our family's Delight into a box, and we gleefully licked our fingers. Oh, how sweet! How special!

"Remember girls," Mom said once we got home. "You have eight pieces each." She looked at us, one at a time. "You can eat them whenever you want, but when they're gone—that's it." We all nodded. We never questioned this, as it was completely fair. No one got more than anyone else, but we each could choose when to eat our share.

Veronita, Denise, and I always ate ours at night, in the bed, under the blanket. In lucky years, we had enough pieces to last about three or four nights—eight or nine pieces each, two or three each night. This was a lucky year! We each carefully picked out one white, one pink, and maybe one green, put them on a plate, and set the plate in the place of honor: the chest of drawers next to the bed, where we could peek at it frequently before bedtime. *No problem getting us to bed on those nights!*

I watched the door click shut and smiled. My sisters didn't even realize Mom had looked in. It was doubly dark: The lights were off, and we were in our blanket tent with its special, mysterious feel. We whispered, we giggled, and we savored the sweet slowly—to make the special pleasure stretch halfway through the night—licking our fingers carefully after each piece of Delight.

While we were in our own little world, enjoying Turkish Delight and each other's company, we told one another what we had bought or made for the others in the family, and wondered aloud what we'd get in return. That night, I sensed somehow that what we were experiencing was a special gift in itself.

Today, when I see boxes of Turkish Delight in specialty shops, my mouth waters and a flutter of anticipation begins. I hear girlish giggles and warm memories flood over me. I am transported back in time to that special place beneath the blanket tent, where whispered secrets and wishes were sacred. I remember the feel of biting into the soft stickiness, reveling in the fact that the Delight would stick to my teeth and perhaps last longer. And, as the sensation of eating something so delightfully special that it entered our home only once a year enveloped me, I realized that, perhaps even more special than the Turkish Delight, was the perfect enjoyment of eating it with my sisters, companionably, in the dark.

Knowing that because we had Turkish Delight in our possession meant our family was wealthy, in all ways that counted, is a good memory—a time of delight—that will bless me forever.

A Different Kind of Carol

BY AMY AMMONS MULLIS

The old two-storied house I grew up in was a multigabled thing with a long porch of uneven boards that covered the entire front, boasting a grand picture window that simply begged for a Christmas tree. Because the house was heated only by fireplaces and cooled by breezes through open windows, Christmas was the only time of year that the living room saw any activity. The rest of the time, it stayed closed and quiet, the stillness and silence waiting for December, when the pop and crackle of burning firewood sounded in the grate. From the inside, the big picture window reflected the firelight like a pictured echo, and from the outside it framed the enchanted glow of our Christmas tree so beautifully it brought tears to my eyes.

Over the years, vivid memories—bits and pieces of storybook Christmases—can still be pulled from my mind as easily as decorations were pulled out of the great wooden trunk in the closet beneath the stairs. I recall with pleasure the simple act of watching Mama put the finishing touches on arrangements of plastic poinsettias and shiny silver balls on the mantelpiece, and tromping through the snow in the front yard to see how the tree looked from outside. After all the decorations were in place, Mom swept the old green carpet to make the tired nap stand up like a rug of soft grass. But my favorite memory is a musical one that rings merrily in my ear from time to time.

In our house, you could expect to hear almost any kind of music. Mama played Gilbert and Sullivan operettas and Beethoven's symphonies on the hi-fi, Daddy played the world's greatest polka tunes and the complete set of Hank Williams's greatest hits from Reader's Digest, and, as time went by, my eldest sister kept us up to date with the latest hits from the Beatles. Best of all, though, were the times Dad would pick up the old guitar that was always within reach beside his favorite chair and strum some tunes from days gone by while he hummed along.

"Sing it. Sing the words!" I'd beg as I swung on the arm of his chair, convinced he made the lyrics up on the spot.

Often, just to tease me, he'd sing a line or two of some silly song he'd picked up in his travels when he'd served on a destroyer in the North Atlantic, and on a submarine in the Pacific in World War II, his eyes twinkling as he waited for the question he knew I would ask.

"Is that a real song?" I'd ask, my brow wrinkled in concentration. "Are you making that up?"

My all-time favorite was "Wabash Cannonball." If I was quiet and pretended I wasn't listening, he'd sing a verse or two and end up with that lively chorus made famous by Roy Acuff years before.

One Christmas, when I was five or perhaps six, the family gathered around the fireplace, holiday cheer wrapped around us like a cozy comforter. We cracked almonds and walnuts from the fruit basket and rescued roasting oranges from the toes of stockings hanging dangerously low on the mantle. Absentmindedly, Daddy pulled out his guitar and leaned back in his chair contentedly, his legs stretched toward the warmth of the fireplace, and began to strum. When he started to sing, I tore my thoughts from Christmas gifts and goodies and scooted toward him, dragging the newest addition to my baby doll family along with me.

I don't have a library of childhood memories that I can call up on demand. As times change and seasons fade, details recoil on shadowy tendrils of half-forgotten thought, but I remember the warmth of the fire on my face that Christmas, and the music that filled the room as Daddy played my favorite ditty on his old guitar. I can see him lounging comfortably, head back and eyes closed, singing the chorus to "Wabash Cannonball" in a clear voice. I remember thinking that I'd better listen with all my might because I never knew when Daddy might sing it all the way through again. And as the last notes trailed into a blend of crackling firewood mixed with the laughter of my brother and sisters, I knew that "Wabash Cannonball" would always be my favorite Christmas carol.

The Lonely Christmas Tree

BY MARILYN JASKULKE

Family fun always meant picking out the Christmas tree together. Boots, mittens, and caps were part of the attire for our snowy adventure in the Midwest. Then off we went: four boys and Mom and Dad all piled into the family sedan in search of the perfect tree.

The sign at the big lot read, "CHRISTMAS TREES FOR SALE." With only a few days left before Christmas, the selection had dwindled. Most of the trees appeared scrawny, not like the lovely full tree we expected to find. But one of the fir trees had a sad and lonely "please take me home" look, which I couldn't resist. I immediately felt bad for the tree and made up my mind it would be that tree or no tree.

"That's it," I piped. "We have to take that one!"

Disgruntled looks appeared on the faces of our sons. They got no sympathy from their father, however, for Cliff understood my heart as much as I did.

"Tie it up on the top of the car," Cliff said without batting an eyelash.

"This was supposed to be fun," my eldest son, DuWayne, muttered as he pulled his stocking cap down over his nose.

The tree shivered and shook on the ride home but arrived minus only a few needles, which was good, because my husband wasn't through with it yet.

"Get the saw," DuWayne said to no one in particular. "And get the metal tree stand, too. We need to get this tree into the water. It doesn't have much time left."

Within minutes, the creative stage had begun. Father and sons began hacking at the lower branches to make it stand straight, something this tree had never done in its life, but their progress was impressive.

"Well . . . let's cut this branch off down here and maybe that will help," Craig—another son—added, looking at me hopefully.

I felt assured this was the right tree for us. Our family had rescued it from being the loneliest tree on the lot. *Who among us wouldn't be proud of that?* The day had been a great adventure and surely this tree would be a symbol of our time spent together.

The tree was tilted once more and returned to the tree stand.

"That's it!" we all chimed at once. Somewhere in the background, I heard the strains of "Oh Christmas Tree," and felt myself exhale happily. My mind raced, thinking of the gifts that would be placed under our perfect Christmas tree, all wrapped in fancy red and green Christmas gift paper.

Then, reality set in. The sad and lonely Christmas tree I had chosen looked sad and lonely no more. It looked completely devastated. And as I looked at my sons, I realized that all interest in decorating the tree had disappeared.

"Let's go outside and make a snow fort," offered one son. In a wink, all four sons were out the door.

Christmas doldrums walked in and replaced the happiness I'd felt only a few minutes earlier. I lost my vision of perfectly wrapped gifts beneath what should have been a sparkling beauty.

Propped in a corner, the tree was left for me to decide its fate.

When Christmas Day arrived, a beautiful tree stood beaming with lights, tinsel, strings of popcorn, and cranberries. All the nostalgic decorations from previous years had been unboxed and hung on each limb, adding a delightful atmosphere to the cozy living room.

It was not the tree we had chosen on our snowy day escapade. The boys and their dad had spent another adventurous day Christmas tree shopping—this time without me. But on their own, they managed to bring home a beauty! It filled the corner of the room, standing tall and handsome.

Visions of sugar plums once again filled my head. The gifts would soon be wrapped and arranged beneath our beautiful new tree. I continued stirring up a batch of gingerbread cookies, now designated for hanging on the tree, rather than placed on a cookie plate.

"Can we eat some of them first?" one child begged.

"Sure, there's more in the oven," I replied with a grin.

"Oh, that's what I smelled when I came in the door," said Cliff. Trying hard to hide the smirk on his face, he asked innocently, "What happened to our other tree?"

I let the smirk go. After all, it was Christmas. I pointed my spoon toward the house next door where our widowed neighbor lived all alone.

"The other day I noticed she didn't have any decorations up. And since I made a wreath out of our first tree, I was wondering if she might like to have it."

Four boys bundled themselves against the cold once more and headed for the neighbor's house. "Would you like to have this Christmas wreath?" the bravest asked.

With tears in her eyes, the elderly woman reached for it. Smiling at the boys, she replied softly, "No one comes to see me at Christmas time. My family is all gone. I don't even have a Christmas tree anymore." She gazed at the wreath with tear-filled eyes. "This is the loveliest most precious wreath I've ever laid eyes on. Will you please help me hang it on my front door?"

"Sure, I will," said our eldest, anxious to help. Shyly, our youngest reached into his pocket and extracted a gingerbread cookie he'd been saving. With no thought to himself, he handed the cookie to his neighbor. Then he smiled, the words "Merry Christmas" spilling from his mouth happily.

The lonely tree, now transformed into a Christmas wreath, had found a home, and in the process, our boys had befriended a lonely soul during what should be the happiest time of the year.

Belonging to Winter

BY FAITH SHERRILL

It was a cold winter for Phoenix, Arizona, and the trees were covered in a thin layer of frost. My grandfather poured himself a fresh cup of coffee and sat down slowly. I watched as he laid his newspaper in front of him and took in an exhausted breath. When he exhaled, his breath extended out into the cold, the puff of air turning white as if a soft cloud had left his chest.

He called me over to sit beside him as we waited for the first customers of the morning. The trees were all lined in horizontal rows, their bowls filled with water, as they, too, waited. A car approached and I sat up a little straighter as Grandpa's sharp blue eyes darted toward the chain-link fence. No luck. They were only trying to turn around in the dirt lot. It was a slow year for selling Christmas trees.

I looked up to Grandpa's tough leathered face and he smiled gently. "They'll be back," he whispered, and I couldn't help returning his smile. In a way, I knew he was right. He had run the Christmas tree lot on that corner for nearly ten years, and when one person left, another always arrived. Grandpa offered me a sip of his black coffee and I shook my head in embarrassment; coffee was not for little girls.

My mother had dropped me off for the day while she ran errands. I didn't mind, though, my grandfather was a little bit of magic—especially around this time of year. I knew if I helped him, he was sure to put in a good word for me with Santa.

I sat patiently, my hands folded in my lap, breathing in the smell of freshly cut trees. He looked down at me and smiled again as he opened his paper. His eyes caught a small article about the boom in the sale of artificial trees that year, and his eyes sagged. I looked up at his white beard and hair and laughed. To me, Grandpa always looked like he belonged to the winter. I reached up and tugged on his whiskers. As I knew he would, he gave a rich belly laugh in return.

"Grandpa . . . can I—" He nodded before I could finish and I rushed out of the chair. I ran through the trees, my imagination taking control. I was running through the forest as wild wolves nipped eagerly at my heels. I turned a sharp corner and barely escaped with my life. I laughed as my little legs moved as quickly as they could.

Then, my imagination turned me into an elf, and I had to inspect every tree to make sure it was worthy enough to go home with a family. I ruffled my fingers through the prickly needles with ease as I pulled one off and held it to my nose. It smelled fresh and wild, new and alive—like me. I dropped the small needle, letting it fall carelessly to the dirt and gravel. As I rounded a corner, I caught sight of another car pulling into the lot. I ran to my grandfather quickly, nearly tumbling headfirst into the few trees.

When I arrived at Grandpa's side, a small tailwind of dirt followed me, dying beneath my small feet. I quickly hopped onto the seat beside him, my chest heaving and my legs throbbing in the cold. I looked up to his face and then into the lot. This car also was just turning around. My head sank as I watched the car disappear down the road. *Who didn't want a tree in the desert; they were so rare?* Grandpa patted my small head as I turned my saddened gaze to his.

"They'll be back," he whispered again, and for a moment, I caught the uncertainty in his voice. I looked at his hands as they trembled with age, his breath heaving wearily out of his chest. I wanted to scream at the cars that passed, to stop them from making a terrible mistake. Couldn't they see that this lot, that this grandpa, was magic? They lived in a desert and they were passing up the chance to find their worth in winter.

I watched Grandpa as the day moved on, slowly. More cars turned and left the small piece of Christmas behind them. Eventually, my mother pulled in and parked just inches before the small opening in the fence. She walked in and I ran to her. I hugged her legs tightly, as if they were breath, as if they were life. She laughed and patted me on the head as she made her way to her father.

"How are they biting this year, Dad?" she asked with a laugh, as she wrapped her arms around his small frame. He looked at me and winked as he stood and returned her embrace.

"Oh, we've been busy all day, and why not, people always need Christmas trees."

With his words, I understood what his wink had meant. I shook my head and kicked the dirt, not sure of what to say as we made our way to Mom's car and climbed in. Grandpa and I waved slowly, sharing the last of the day with one another. Then Mom turned the car around and we drove off, leaving Grandpa in the dirt with his trees.

That special time with Grandpa was destined to be one of our last times together at the tree lot. I think back on his blue eyes, his white beard and hair, and I don't feel the chill of winter at all. Instead, warmth radiates in my chest.

I still visit the old lot, even though it's empty now. I still imagine the wolves are chasing me, and I need to inspect every tree to make sure they're worthy of the little children that will camp around them. Sometimes I even imagine pulling a needle from one of their long branches and holding it to my nose, but not to smell the tree; I do it to breathe in my grandfather, and all of the love he brought with him to give out to the people who stopped and stayed for a while.

I think about what he was really offering out there on that small lot. I think about how I miss him, as well as all of the friends and family I've lost over the years. I know now that his words were true, "They'll be back." One day, I will see him again. Somewhere past winter and beyond spring, we'll all find each other, and when we do, we'll all come back to Christmas.

Finding Santa

BY DEBRA J. RANKIN

It had been one of those dreary winter days when kids are home from school for Christmas break. Bored with entertaining my two-year-old brother, Stevie, I went looking for my older brother, Kenny, who had told me the other day that there was no Santa. Kenny didn't like me hanging around all the time. He was good at hiding from me, but I was even better at finding him.

Wandering into the kitchen, I noticed the basement door was slightly ajar. We hadn't lived in this big old house very long and I had never been in the basement before. I pushed timidly at the door. It creaked open and cool damp air touched my face. I squinted into the darkness. Shadows moved across the steps. The wooden stairs weren't welcoming, and the floor at the bottom was hardly visible. No noise came from the basement. *Why would Kenny be down there?*

I held the railing with both hands and started to sneak down the stairs, sliding my hands along the railing as I moved. I heard a scuffling sound and hesitated as the furnace rumbled to life. I shuddered and gripped the railing tighter. I didn't dare call out to Kenny; it would be just like him to hide and then jump out and scare me. Instead, I waited quietly until the furnace settled down.

Halfway down the stairs, I saw the gray cinderblock walls and gray floor that seemed to suck the light from the bare bulb hanging from the ceiling. I stepped onto the cold cement floor in my stocking feet and shivered.

My brother was balancing on a Big Tonka truck with his back to me, at the workbench. He was so engrossed in whatever he was doing, that he looked like Frankenstein in his laboratory.

I tiptoed closer. "What ya doin' down here?" I asked.

Kenny jumped at the sound of my voice. Then he spun around and leapt off the truck. With outstretched arms, he moved toward me.

"Get out of here!" he shouted. "You can't come down here!"

Startled, I took one step backward and tilted my head up to look him in the eye. Kenny blocked my view of the workbench with his arms, so I tried to duck beneath them, but he was too quick for me.

"Get out of here!" he shouted again.

I frowned. "What ya doin' down here?"

Kenny grabbed me and tried to push me toward the stairs. "It's a secret."

I loved it when Kenny had secrets—it usually meant he wasn't supposed to be doing what he was doing.

I tried to wiggle free of his grip.

"No!" he shouted. "Go back upstairs!"

I knew if I left I would never find out what Kenny was doing, so I stood with my feet frozen to the floor like, little Cindy-Lou Who staring down the Grinch.

Finally, he relented. "You gotta promise you won't tell anybody—even Mom."

"Okay. I promise."

Kenny leaned toward me and whispered, "Come here, I'll show you." I stepped up on the Tonka Truck and gazed at the workbench.

"Wow!" I breathed.

Sitting on the workbench was Kenny's old wooden train set, a glass of water, and a set of water colors. It looked just like Santa's workshop! Kenny had carefully sanded the cars and was adding matching paint to the chipped areas.

"I'm fixing it up nice for Stevie. For Christmas," he explained.

Kenny didn't need to say anything else. He was thinking of someone besides himself! He was fixing up his well-loved train set to give to our little brother for Christmas. My big brother—the one who told me there was no Santa—was working very hard at *being* Santa, and that made me smile.

The Baby Jesus Bed

BY KATHLEEN M. MULDOON

"Hurry, Gran," I urged, as my grandmother followed me off the rickety elevator and into the basement of our apartment building.

It was the first Sunday in Advent and time to retrieve the Baby Jesus bed from our storage bin. I'd always felt unsafe in the musty cellar, but today, now that I was ten, I felt braver as we wound through the maze of chicken-wire enclosures that held the tenants' surplus belongings. Finally, we reached the bin marked 8B.

As Gran turned the key in the padlock, I noticed something strange. A hole had been cut in the chicken wire on one side of our bin, and it looked as though stuff had been pulled from some of our boxes. I pointed it out to Gran.

"Why, honey, we've got nothing anyone would want," Gran said.

She grunted as she pulled open the warped doorframe and we stepped inside. It soon became apparent that someone had at least thought they wanted our stuff, because sure enough, several items were missing. Among them was the cardboard box that held our meager Christmas decorations, including the miniature wooden manger I called the Baby Jesus bed.

The first Christmas I remember seeing it was in 1952, the year I turned five. Gran had brought it and a Jesus figurine with her from Ireland when she'd immigrated to the United States during the Great Depression. As had been her family tradition, she taught me that the amount of straw that would fill the little manger depended on my behavior during Advent. My good deeds and good school grades earned ten pieces of straw each, which I placed in the manger every night. On Christmas Eve, I solemnly placed the Infant statue atop the straw. Some Christmases, I'm sorry to say, Jesus had a mighty slim mattress.

"Look!" Gran cried.

On the floor, where the ornament box had been stored, was the statue of the infant Jesus. The fall had broken off one leg, which lay beside it.

"It's a miracle," Gran whispered as she reached down reverently to pick up the statue. "It must have fallen out of the box when the thief pulled it through the hole."

Cradling the Baby Jesus in her apron, we rode the elevator back up to our flat. Gran seemed delighted to have found the statue, but I was furious. *How dare someone steal our box? More importantly, where would the Infant lay His head?* I felt as though our whole Christmas was ruined. Not only had the thieves stolen Jesus's bed, our Christmas ornament box had also held the bag of straw we used every year.

After Gran glued the statue back together and put it on a towel to dry, she emptied the cardboard box that held wooden matches to light the burners on our stove.

"This will do for our manger," she said.

"But what about the straw?" I whined.

Gran grabbed shears and trimmed pieces of straw from our whisk broom and handed them to me.

"These will do," she said.

Suddenly, I couldn't hold back my tears. The pretty Baby Jesus bed had been made by my great-grandfather. I'd never met him, but Gran had often told me the story of how he whittled it himself. The matchbox with "Diamond" printed on the side hardly seemed a suitable replacement for Jesus.

Gran hugged me. "Hush now, you know it upsets your mother when you cry."

I looked at my mother, sitting in the same chair she always sat in. She looked like a statue herself, her eyes vacant and staring. I'd never known her to be well. She was just "Mom," who Gran and I dressed, fed, and led to her chair each day. I almost wished my crying would upset her so she'd seem more like a real person to me.

Angrily, I swiped at my tears and leaped up. "I'm going to write a letter," I announced. "I'm going to ask the thief to bring back the Baby Jesus bed."

Gran shook her head. "Folks who steal don't care about making things right," she said.

But I wrote my letter anyway. I don't remember the exact words I printed on that paper, but I remember how I addressed it. "To the person who stole the Christmas box from 8B." In a sentence or two, I explained about the Baby Jesus bed and how important it was for our Christmas. Then I got the building manager to let me tape my letter by the mailboxes in the lobby.

Slowly, the days of Advent passed. Each night, I dutifully placed my pieces of straw in the matchbox, but my heart wasn't in it. I tried to sound cheerful when I read our Christmas cards to Mom, but the loss of the Jesus bed had changed the way I looked at the holiday. Gran, too, was only going through the motions as she baked her shamrock cookies for neighbors, the mailman, and the milkman. This Christmas just wasn't the same without our Baby Jesus bed in the center of the kitchen table, awaiting the reception of the statue on Christmas Eve.

By the time Christmas approached, the matchbox was bursting with straw. On the night before Christmas, Gran prepared our usual Christmas Eve soup, and the smell of ginger-bread filled our apartment. I had just led Mom to the kitchen table when I thought I heard something brush against our apartment door. Gran heard it, too.

"Go and see," she said. "Don't take the chain off, though."

I went to the door, stood on my tiptoes, and peered through the peephole. I didn't see anyone in the hallway. Cautiously, I opened the door as much as the security chain allowed. I still didn't see anyone. I was about to close the door when I noticed a paper sack on the floor. It had "8B" written on it in pencil. I grabbed it and pulled it inside.

"It's for us!" I said. "Should I look inside?"

"Better let me," Gran said as she pinned a towel around Mom's neck.

Gran took off the tape that held the bag shut and gasped. With a shaking hand, she pulled out our Baby Jesus bed! A tear trickled down her face. Even Mom seemed to notice that something very special was happening. Gran searched further in the bag and found a piece of paper. It was the note I'd taped to the wall downstairs. On it, someone had written the words "I'M SORRY."

After we ate supper, Gran helped me transfer the straw from the matchbox to the little wooden manger. After I had lifted the Baby Jesus statue and carefully placed it on the straw, Gran, Mom, and I held hands. Gran offered a prayer of thanksgiving, both for the birth of our Savior and for the return of the manger, that, for us, symbolized His coming. When I opened my eyes again, I saw a tiny smile on Mom's face. Happiness from that little smile spilled from her into me, and I knew this would be the best Christmas of my life. And it was.

Through the Innocence of Childhood

BY BARBARA JEANNE FISHER

The trouble with some of us is that we have been inoculated with small doses of commercialized Christmas, with presents and Santa and monetary treasures, and that keeps us from catching the "real thing." Perhaps I was even a little bit that way, until one winter evening, when my husband and I decided to take our grandchildren down to our cabin in the woods for an evening of preseason fun together.

Sitting on a giant rug, surrounded by children, I read them the traditional story of Christmas. I told them about Mary and Joseph arriving in Bethlehem. I explained to them that finding no room in the inn, the couple went to a stable, where Baby Jesus was born and placed in a manger. Throughout the story, the children sat in amazement, trying to grasp every word.

When I finished reading the story, the children asked questions while we drank hot chocolate and ate frosted Christmas cookies. When they finished eating, I gave them each several pieces of construction material to make a crude manger. I instructed them to think about Baby Jesus and the first Christmas, and make a nativity scene from the items they were given.

The children were so creative! Following my simple instructions, they began tearing the paper and carefully laying strips of it in the manger for straw. Small squares of flannel were used as a blanket for Baby Jesus. A doll-like baby was cut from tan felt.

All went well, until I got to the table where little six-year-old Brianna sat. I knew she was going through a hard time understanding life and the harshness that oftentimes accompanies it, because several times she had mentioned her friend Brian's sadness over his parent's divorce. She talked of little else these days. Today, as I looked at her sweet innocent face, I saw the sadness still mirrored there.

Looking down at the table, I was surprised to see two infants in the manger.

"Does Jesus have a friend in the manger with Him today?" I asked.

Crossing her little arms stubbornly, Brianna looked at her completed manger scene and very seriously began to explain. For such a young child, who had only heard the Christmas story a few times, she related the happenings accurately—until she came to the part where Mary put Baby Jesus in the manger. Then Brianna started to ad lib. She made up her own ending to the story.

" . . . and when Mary laid the baby in the manger, Jesus looked at my friend Brian, and asked him if he had a place to stay," Brianna explained carefully. "He told Jesus that his mommy and daddy had just gotten a divorce and were fighting over who would get to keep him, and so he didn't have any place to live. Then Jesus told Brian that he could stay with Him. But he told Jesus that he couldn't, because he didn't have a gift to give Him like everybody else did.

"Brian wanted to stay with Jesus so much, so he thought and thought about what he could use for a gift. He knew it was cold in the manger, so he figured if maybe he could keep Jesus warm, then that would be a good gift.

"Brian said, 'If I lay real close to you so you are not cold, will that be a good enough gift?'

"Jesus smiled. He said, 'If you keep me warm, that will be the best gift anybody ever gave me.' So, Brian climbed up into the manger and cuddled close to Jesus, who told him he could stay with Him—for always."

As little Brianna finished her story, her eyes brimmed full of tears, then splashed down her little cheeks. "Grandma, isn't that great? My friend Brian found someone who would never abandon nor abuse him again, someone who would stay with him—FOR ALWAYS!"

I nodded and held Brianna close. No words were necessary. Through the innocent eyes of childhood, not only had Brianna already found the "real thing" nestled in and amongst the gifts and presents and commercialization of Christmas, she had also figured out how to share it.

The Christmas Tree Hunter

BY ANN HITE

If a family photo existed from the Christmas of 1968, it would have captured a time and place I can only return to in my mind. The picture would be black and white and crinkled around the edges. Mom, in her bright red sweater, blonde hair curled around her face, would watch Dad and me with a nervous smile. I'd be dressed in the glorious red, green, and black plaid jumper Mom had made me that season. Dad, solid and dependable, standing behind us dressed in his military fatigues, would wear a stern look. But, at the last minute, just as the camera clicked, a half smile would appear.

Two days before that Christmas Eve, Dad had watched the morning news. He had stared at the black and white twenty-five-inch screen—the best in the neighborhood—as if he were already part of the jungle scenes. There were young soldiers carrying guns and wearing helmets, smoking cigarettes, and grinning into the camera—part of the televised war taking place in Vietnam, and it all panned out before him. This morning, however, he wasn't watching the television. Instead, he was huffing around like maybe he hadn't used his best judgment.

Mom had somehow talked Dad into taking me with him that morning.

As we tamped in snow high enough to slide inside my tall boots, I insisted the air smelled like icicles. Dad said there was no such odor, but I was sure I detected a clean, faintly sweet fragrance that only icicles could give. I never uttered a word about my cold feet, even as my toes began to tingle.

Our mission: search out the perfect tree and bring it home.

Dad, a lifer in the Air Force, worked at all tasks with the same dogged determination as he must have used marching to the front during World War II. And now, as we hunted for the perfect tree, it was as if we were stationed in Germany on his second tour of duty, for that was the way Dad approached all things.

The woods were dense, but bright due to the snow that coated everything with pure light. I imagined the ice crystals falling from the higher branches were fairies dancing to music of their own. I joined in their dance, a ballerina twirling and leaping, until Dad turned and glared at me.

"Quiet." He spoke in a loud whisper as he pointed in front of us.

The tree, the best tree ever, sat in a clearing, as if the other trees had stepped back to give her—I knew it was a girl—room to grow round and full, thick with short needles. She was shorter than all the other trees, which only made her more appealing, especially to a Christmas tree hunter like my dad.

I pointed to the branches where the snow had settled in clumps. "Can't we take her home just like this?" I wished aloud.

Dad made the sound he always made when he thought I had silly thoughts in my head. He mumbled under his breath as he circled the tree, leaving large footprints in the snow. I followed, placing my boots into each print. When he stopped, I ran into his back.

He turned with a frown on his face. "Careful."

He held the bow saw in one hand and studied his prize with serious concentration, like a master builder about to choose his first cut. After much chin rubbing and muttering, he squatted for a long look. After what seemed like an eternity, he cut into the tree trunk. I swore I heard a sigh of pain, a sadness released into the air. When I told him this, he shook his head.

"Ann," he said sternly, "you have your head full of dreams." Somehow, his voice remained soft and firm at the same time.

He made a clean cut through the bark, sawing with a speed that caused tiny pieces of wood to fly. I turned my head and thought instead of strands of lights and strings of popcorn.

In great detail, I described the decorations I would hang on this special tree: glass ornaments handed down from one generation to another, the blue beads, and the red-haired angel with golden wings. "She protects us," I explained.

My comment brought a half smile that smoothed the lines around Dad's mouth.

His combat boots trudged off, leading his tall frame away from the attack scene. The tree dragged behind him, clearing a path through the forest, which I felt privileged to step into.

As we continued on our mission, each tree became a hiding place for the enemy, and I instructed Dad to keep low so their fire wouldn't hit us or damage our prize, the perfect Christmas tree. We snaked our way through the woods, one careful step at a time, back into the bright daylight of another world, our world, if only for a while.

We tugged the tree, hands touching, through the snow, past the silent deserted playground, now covered with a blanket of white.

The sun rode the sky with little warmth, but still the icicles began to fade, one drip at a time. My feet had gone numb long before this business of dragging the tree home, and now clumsiness set in as we worked our way down the hill toward our yard. We left the tree outside the backdoor and entered the warm steamy house, the aroma of banana bread reminding me how hungry I was. Mother looked up from the piecrust she was rolling. I hoped it would be a pumpkin pie.

As I watched her look at Dad, I knew this would be the perfect Christmas, this last Christmas before Dad received his tour in Vietnam. Oh, there would be time again—after Dad returned home safely—for more Christmas tree hunting missions, but I knew nothing would ever be as magical as this year's Christmas tree hunt had been. And nothing ever was.

Disappearing Act

BY RANDY JEAN BRUSKRUD

When I was a little girl, Santa Claus always made house calls on Christmas Eve, bringing his round-bellied cheer, along with gifts for my brother and me. On those December nights, as the scent of roasting turkey filled the kitchen and arriving relatives crowded the family room with excited chatter, I had but one goal: to keep track of my father's whereabouts. My reason being, somehow, every year, he managed to miss Santa's visit.

"We're out of film for the camera," he'd say. "I'll just zip downtown and be back in no time. I promise."

Meanwhile, Santa came and went while Daddy was gone.

"We need cream for the coffee, honey," he'd shout into the living room from the kitchen, his hand already on the doorknob. "It'll only take twenty minutes for a run to the grocery store."

Meanwhile, Santa came and went while Daddy was gone.

Year after year, no matter how hard I tried to keep him home and in my line of vision, my father thwarted my efforts every time.

This Christmas would be different, I vowed.

"Where are you going?" I demanded as he headed toward the rear of the house.

"To the bathroom," he whispered with a sheepish grin that failed to fool me.

"No way! Use the one off the kitchen," I suggested. "It's closer to the front door and if Santa arrives, you'll hear him."

"Ah," he said as he switched course. "Good idea."

I waited outside the door, tapping my foot, confident in my plan.

"Leave your father in peace," my mom said from the kitchen as she basted the turkey.

"I can't," I insisted stubbornly. "It's almost time for Santa to get here, and I don't want Daddy to miss him again!"

She sighed, brushed a lock of hair from her forehead, and eyed me wearily. "Don't argue, honey. I need you to set the table."

Well, I could hardly disobey. Reluctantly, I headed for the dining room with plates and silverware. As I positioned each knife with its blade pointing in and lined up the forks and spoons with careful precision, I thought about my conversations with Santa at the mall. This year, I'd asked for a Patty Playmate doll—a doll nearly as big as me that I could dress in my own clothes. I was concerned about whether Santa would be able to fit her in his sleigh, and was glad he didn't have to bring her down our chimney.

About five minutes later, I heard a loud pounding on the front door. I gave a moment's thought to rousting my dad from the bathroom, but decided I couldn't keep Santa waiting outside in the chilly December air.

Daddy had managed to be "gone" again. But as Santa's booming presence filled the living room, I quickly forgot Dad's absence. Santa was explaining something about not being able to bring the gift I'd requested and I didn't want to miss a word of it.

"We were all out of Patty Paige dolls," he said solemnly, "but I brought you something else I hope you'll like."

Patty Paige dolls? Did Santa mean Patty Playmate? Daddy always said Patty Paige doll, too. Funny how they both made the same mistake, I thought in surprise. Glancing down at Santa's shoes, I realized they were the same kind of shoes Daddy wore, too! Feeling a rush of pride that such an important man shared so much in common with my own father, I smiled.

As I stared in awe at Santa, I suddenly remembered something. "Mommy, where's that new suit for Santa? Don't you want to give it to him?" She seemed to pale. "You know. The one I found in your closet. You said Santa needed an extra one."

Santa, however, was too busy to wait. "I'll get it next year," he assured me. "I have to go now, because my next stop's a long way from here. I'm off to North Dakota to visit a little girl named Lindsay Larson."

My mouth dropped open. "That's my cousin!" I exclaimed. *I mean, what were the odds?* I was truly amazed.

With a final rendition of "Ho-Ho-Ho," Santa departed, and my brother and I settled in to open the packages he'd brought. I was so involved with my presents I didn't even notice when Daddy came out of the bathroom.

Christmas Giving

BY LINDA KAULLEN PERKINS

As the lime green 1950 Chevy crawled backward, I knew Daddy's eyes were shifting from the rearview mirror to the side mirrors. Normally, I would be helping him park the car from the backseat, saying things like, "Don't get too close to the curb, Daddy" or "Did you see that black car back there?" Today, I was too busy to offer the wisdom of a six year old.

My fingers dipped into the coin purse. "One, two . . . " I counted in a whisper. My heart quickened. What if, somehow, a quarter had slithered behind the sofa cushions unnoticed when I had counted the change earlier? Thoughts of a thieving couch worried me. No one suspected the worn sofa as a change gobbler, until it was turned upside down to fit through the front door and coins showered in every direction.

"Three, four, five," I finished counting. With my allowance piled high in one hand, I breathed a sigh of relief. Five quarters had been there earlier this morning and five were there when I counted right before we left the house. Nothing had happened to my precious savings on the drive to town.

"Whoa, Nellie," Daddy said to the car, turning off the key.

I giggled at Daddy and scooted toward the door.

He winked at me. "I'll wait here while you two shop," he said.

Mama put some money in the parking meter and I slammed the car door.

"Woolworth's will have what you're looking for," Mama said, nodding in the direction of the dime store.

"I can only spend a quarter for the girl's gift," I reminded her.

"Yes," she said, reaching for the brass handle of the heavy door. The wooden floor creaked as we stepped inside and the aroma of cooking food made my stomach growl. Somebody had probably ordered one of those big juicy hamburgers, and a thick chocolate malt. I squeezed my arms across my stomach.

"Do you feel okay?" Mama asked.

I nodded. "That food smells so good."

"We're having hamburgers for supper tonight," she said, slipping a shopping basket over her arm.

We walked up and down the aisles, past the hairnets, Pond's cold cream, white gloves, garters, and nylon stockings. Then Mama stopped in front of a counter stacked with thin boxes. "These might make good presents for your teacher," she said, showing me the contents.

"But she likes perfume," I whined.

"Do you know what kind to buy?" Mama's studied me with loving brown eyes.

I shrugged. "Maybe I *should* get the handkerchiefs. What about the blue ones?"

"I think those are very nice." Mama smiled. "They're in a box and will be easy to wrap. But," she tapped me on the nose with her finger, "it will take three of your quarters."

"Okay." I sighed. "At least I don't have to spend a whole dollar."

"Where shall we look for the girl's gift?" Mama asked.

"The toy aisle!" I shouted, hurrying ahead of Mama up the ramp into the toy section.

"If I knew who would get the present, it would be easier," I complained.

"True." Mama nodded. "But sometimes," she paused and looked at me, "the person who needs your gift most will get it."

I didn't understand Mama's thinking. The teacher would number all the girl's presents and then we would draw numbers. Each gift would go with the matching number. The teacher would do the same for the boys. How could anyone possibly get the present they needed?

I fingered the book with paper dolls. "I could buy this."

"Look around a bit," Mama advised. "You don't want to buy the first thing you see. Lots of things here cost a quarter. I see jump ropes, jacks, puzzles, and checkers."

"Here's a dress-up kit. It has real high heels and play lipstick."

"How much is it?" Mama asked.

"Fifty cents." I frowned and put it back, and picked up another item. "Mama, look! A Tiny Tears doll! You can put water in her bottle and she cries real tears. If I could only buy her for one of the girls," I moaned. "But she costs way too much."

"Look here," Mama said. "You can get these two things for a quarter."

A coloring book and crayons didn't quite compare to the doll, but that's what I ended up carrying to the cash register. With quarters cupped in my hand, I offered them to the sales clerk.

"I'll pay the sales tax," Mama said, handing the clerk several pennies.

Heaviness filled me at the loss of my coveted money. It must have shown on my face because Mama patted my shoulder.

"Remember, it is better to give than to receive," she said softly. I nodded, fisting the bag in one hand. It crinkled and slapped against my pocket with the lone quarter, reminding me that my money was nearly gone and yet consoling me at the same time.

Back at home, I couldn't wait to wrap the gifts. Smiling at my eagerness, Mama took a filled shopping bag out of the closet.

"I've saved this paper from last year, and it's full of wrinkles," she said.

Disappointed at the colorful but wrinkled paper, I whined, "But, Mama, I want the presents to look nice."

"That's why I'm setting up the ironing board," she said patiently. "Go look in the kitchen closet for a box for the coloring book and crayons."

"Why do I need a box? I can wrap them like this."

She raised her eyebrows as she looked at me. "You don't want it to look sloppy. A gift should be like an honorable person—good on the inside and tidy in appearance."

When I thought about it, I had to agree.

Just as she said, the ironed paper looked good as new as Mama wrapped and taped and snipped. She turned the package upside down and showed me from beginning to end how to make the package tidy.

"The ends will be a little harder to do," she explained as she got to the last part. "First, I'll push this top piece down and then fold the sides in like this. Make sharp creases with your hand. Bring the bottom piece up and tape. Now you do the other end." She slid the package in front of me.

I pushed the top piece down. She scooted close to me and said, "Fold it right there." I did what she said, but my side didn't look as neat as hers.

She cut a length of ribbon and wrapped it around the gift. "Put your finger there while I tie the knot," she said. Leaning close, she smiled, "Sometimes, it takes two people to do a job." After she tied the bow, she showed me how to run the ribbon over the scissor blade to make it curl.

I stared in awe at the tidy package in front of me. "It looks beautiful, Mama! But," I added wistfully, "I still wish it had a Tiny Tears doll inside."

"Well, the girl that gets this might *need* a new coloring book and crayons," she said.

A surprising thing happened the day of the Christmas party: The girl who got my gift showed me the broken crayons in her desk. "I've been begging Mom for some new ones," she said, her eyes sparkling. "Thanks!"

As if helium balloons were tied to my toes, I skipped home. "Mama," I yelled happily, yanking open the front door, "she needed the crayons!"

Mama smiled, leaning down to hug me as I barreled into her arms. "See!" she said, grinning. "She got the right present!"

Many years later, I realize how blessed I was to receive Mama's gifts of love and wisdom. She took every opportunity to teach me about life—whether it was about giving gifts, accepting gifts from others, or plainly and simply doing the right thing. But mostly, Mama showed me how to live—and that's the best gift any mother can pass on to her children.

The Empty Chair

BY DELBERT L. BIEBER

There was an empty chair at the kitchen table on Christmas day, and I could not help but stare at it and wonder. In the 1950s, the kitchen table was the hub of family life. Well, at least it was on our farm. The kitchen table was where we all met at least once every day, most days twice, and quite often thrice.

The kitchen table was where we shared soup, broke bread, devoured roasts, and savored pie. It was where we licked our fingers and our wounds. It was where we prayed and laughed and cried together, told the stories of our lives, and learned the history of our heritage. It was where we learned to laugh at ourselves and with each other.

The kitchen table always had enough space for one more. It was where we entertained guests and strangers, who were no longer strangers at meal's end. It was where the extended family gathered on holidays and where the preacher sat when he came to visit.

Between meals, the kitchen table was where we pretended to do our homework while we played dots and tic-tactoe. It was where the insurance man spread the papers from his briefcase beside a cup of coffee and a piece of pie. It was where Mom and Dad read us the Bible before bedtime. And it was where we received backrubs and hair cuts.

Cataract blindness and a broken hip ended Granny's attendance at the kitchen table. She couldn't descend the stairs anymore and come to the kitchen table—not for breakfast, not for lunch, not for supper. And now, on this Christmas day, I just stared at her empty chair and imagined she was still there.

I had already taken Granny's meal to her bedside, just like I did every day, just like I would continue to do. Mom always fixed a tray of soft foods of bran flakes or oatmeal for breakfast, soup or a soft-boiled egg for lunch, and tiny pieces of meat, mashed potatoes, and well-cooked vegetables for supper. Sometimes she made a special treat of shoo fly pie and ice cream.

Each time I carried the tray into Granny's bedroom, she apologized for the inconvenience. I'm not sure I ever convinced her, but to serve her was not an inconvenience. It was an honor.

Sometimes she asked me to read her passages from the Bible while she ate. Sometimes she asked me to tell her what was happening on the farm. Sometimes she asked me to look out of her window and describe the view. Sometimes I just sat in the big over-stuffed chair in the corner and marveled at the beauty that came from somewhere beneath her wrinkled skin and clouded eyes. Sometimes she told me stories about her twelve children, the friends she had lost through two world wars, and sometimes she talked about the Great Depression and how she fed the hobos who came from the rail yard. During our talks, she told me about her own childhood and growing up on the farm with seventeen brothers and sisters. Once in a while, she would sing a little song in Pennsylvania Dutch and then translate it into Dutch-English for me. And when she told me how proud she was of all her grandchildren, I sat a little taller in the overstuffed chair.

In time, the portions on her tray shrank.

As the weeks passed and her strength waned, I put a little stool beside her bed, where I sat and helped guide the spoon to her mouth. Later, she just let me handle the spoon, the cup, and the napkin myself. There were fewer conversations now, more silence, less singing, more reflection.

That morning as I leaned over to place the familiar kiss of departure on her forehead, she stroked my face with her bony, wrinkled hands. The mystery of innocent love reached across the chasm of the generations and connected our souls one more time. In that instant, I knew Granny would soon leave the farm altogether for a better place. But now, moments later on this crisp Christmas morning, as I looked at the chair at the kitchen table now empty of Granny's presence, I almost smiled. Granny's presence wasn't gone. I knew where it was. It was in my heart, and I knew it would always be there.

The Stranger with the Cardboard Suitcase

BY SHIRLEY P. GUMERT

It was my grandma, my dad's mother, who had bought the brightly colored inexpensive print of "The Last Supper" that hung above the old sideboard, next to my parents' oak dining table. Pictorial Jesus and his Twelve Apostles observed every meal prepared in my parents' kitchen, heard every blessing, saw all our family gatherings. Feasts my mother and aunts set out at Christmastime surely must have astonished those staid images. Sometimes, our laughter did indeed shake the mirrored frame that held the picture.

At Christmastime, foods and desserts covered the sideboard. And always, in the center of everything, stood a cake stand topped by a four-layer, lighter-than-air, white cake with white seven-minute icing and all the grated coconut that would stick to it. That cake was my dad's favorite Christmas dessert.

After all these years, I am the one who ended up with the tall cake stand. And though I seldom bake a coconut cake, I have many memories that revolve around my precious cake stand.

As I think about Christmas, one special memory from the 1960s comes to mind.

Christmas was in full swing—the hugging, comparing, sharing. We'd opened gifts, walked down to the pond and back, and waited for aunts and uncles to bring still more food—until bowls covered even the washer and dryer, and Dad had to find extra chairs to accommodate everyone. Then we feasted, family style.

Eventually, every plate was clean, clear down to the blue Currier-and-Ives patterns. Well, a few of us hid our helpings of turnips—our grandmother's favorite vegetable. When we were down to just the womenfolk and a few children in the kitchen, with one aunt brewing coffee and another two washing and drying dishes, Mom began to reminisce.

"We have so much now," said Mom. "It's not like other years—those War years when we couldn't get sugar to make pies. We made raisin pies, though, and ribbon cane syrup pies, and we had our house full of young soldiers from the base over at Tyler. For that day, at least, they were our family."

She shook her head as she remembered, wondering where the time had flown.

"It's not like Depression days now," Mom continued. "When we had hobo after hobo drop off from freight trains and find their ways to our back door, to ask for any kind of food. We shared what we had, usually vegetables we grew and canned ourselves, or biscuits with bacon stuck inside. We had Christmas, though."

Mom's recollections were interrupted by Dad, who entered the kitchen in a rush. We all looked up expectantly.

"There's a young man—walking, hitchhiking," he explained. "He says he's on his way to a buddy's place. Says the buddy has found a job for him—if he can get there in time." He shook his head. "Says he'll gladly pay for a meal—humph!—like we'd take money for food! He's not eaten all day. No café's open on Christmas Day. He won't come in—says he's dusty from the road."

Long before Dad finished the story, Mom had already begun filling a plate. Her eyes sparkled. She pulled leftovers out of the refrigerator and urged aunts to find "tastes" of every good thing available.

"He can come in," she added. "He's welcome here in our house."

"He says he'll wait outside, with us men," said Dad, as he poured a tall jar of sweetened tea, and then found napkins and cutlery.

I watched as one of my aunts filled a plate with desserts and then put the entire meal on a plastic tray—the one with a poinsettia print—and took the food out.

Leaning against a fencepost, near the highway, the young man sat on his suitcase, soaking up sunshine. Dad handed the tray to the stranger, and later told us how hungry the man must have been.

"He sure liked that food—all that food," Dad said, adding, "I'd accidentally put two pieces of coconut cake onto his tray, so I helped him eat that." Knowing how much Dad enjoyed coconut cake, we all grinned. "He was real pale skinned, thin, looked like he'd slept in those clothes. I offered him a jacket, a cap, whatever he needed, but he wouldn't take anything."

"Where was he from?" asked my grandmother. "Around here?"

"Well, he did like the sweet potato pie and turnips, so I guess he knew something," Dad teased. "Several of us offered him a ride, but he said he'd catch a lift—hitchhike—did not want to bother us."

My mom made a small cry. "Bother? It's Christmas! He came here to us, and it's Christmas!"

"Well, he didn't have much, but he did keep up some pride," Dad said. "He shook my hand firmly. He said 'Thank you. Tell all who made this meal, thank you.' I told him to come back some day, and let us know how the world's treating him in his new job, when he's among friends.

"He just smiled, and he walked out by the highway with his suitcase in hand. He walked up the road a little way, and he put out his thumb to hitchhike. He didn't walk more than a hundred yards when a trucker stopped to pick him up. I guess the trucker figured it was the right thing to do at Christmas."

While Dad relayed the story, I sat beside the table, looking up at the picture of Jesus and his Twelve Apostles. I swear Jesus smiled. Then I looked at the remnants of our family feast and saw the last of the coconut cake on the cake stand. It suddenly appeared more elegant than any other cake on any other Christmas Day, and I was filled with joy to be part of a family that included a woman who made the best coconut cake and a man who knew how to share his coconut cake with a stranger.

Giving and Receiving

BY CLAUDIA MCKINNEY MUNDELL

We stood in the Singer store, our rubber boots leaving little puddles of melted snow on the showroom floor. Gran and Mom gazed longingly at a sewing machine wrapped under a bright-red velvet bow while we waited patiently.

"Mother, you could so use this machine for Christmas!" declared Mom. "Your old machine is going to the shop much too often these days."

Though Mom sewed us simple sundresses and corduroy pants when she had time, it was her own mother who was the family seamstress. Gran made our Easter dresses, winter coats, Halloween costumes, swimwear, and whatever the latest style she found in the McCall's or Simplicity pattern books. She sewed us pinafores and neon-colored skirts layered with miles of rickrack. Occasionally, she even stitched our dolls outfits that matched our own.

Gran ran her hand longingly over the Model 401, heavy with sturdy beige metal parts. "It has discs that allow all kinds of decorative stitches. I could even monogram the girls' dresses if I had this machine," she fantasized out loud. "I am getting tired of fighting that old machine, begging it to sew."

Then she glanced down at us girls who were listening, but were anxious to move on to the Kress Five and Dime Store. "Well, we will see. Christmas is only a few weeks away, and Grandpa said he had something very special for me this year—that he splurged on me. Maybe this is it."

She smiled down at us. "Now, who wants to look at the painted turtles in the dime store?" Nodding happily, we grabbed her hand and helped move her toward the door. "Anyone for hot cashews?" she asked. We nodded again, more than ready.

Gran had barely finished our red plaid satin Christmas dresses that year when her old machine jammed up and had to be hauled in for yet another repair, just four days before Christmas. With black velvet collars and cuffs, the dresses were ready except for buttons and hems, which Gran did by hand. Mom helped with the handwork, hemming one dress while Gran worked on the other.

"I hope Dad knows to shop at the Singer store, Mother," Mom said under her breath so that Grandpa wouldn't hear. "Surely, he realizes what you truly wanted this year." As they talked hopefully about Grandpa's promise of something special, both yearned passionately for that Singer Zig-Zag to be under the tree.

But when we arrived early Christmas Eve to pick up our grandparents for Midnight Mass, Gran had opened her special gift already. The gift had not come in a big box and was not the much-needed sewing machine. Instead, Gran was wearing a mink stole! It was beautiful and soft, luxurious and rich. Grandpa had splurged all right. Thinking he had chosen well, he was proud of his purchase. Gran wore it to Mass, along with an appreciative but weak smile.

Our mom was peeved with her dad for spending so much on a frivolous item when the sewing machine was needed and so wanted, but she didn't say anything to him. Instead, she cornered Gran. "How could he do this?" she snipped in her loudest hushed voice, as we all marched out the door and into the crisp night.

"Shhh," Gran replied, her smile ever present. "He does not need to know I'm disappointed."

"But we all dropped hints and he knows your sewing machine is always broken," Mom pressed.

"Yes, but he *needed* to give me this," Gran explained. "This is what he thinks any woman would want. He thinks he has done well—answered a woman's dream. Let him have that for Christmas."

Gran never complained. She wore the fur on a few isolated occasions and then left it stored most of the time on a shelf in the closet. Occasionally, when we begged to see the mink, she took it down. When we were in high school, we borrowed it for our proms. We were certainly overdressed for a Kansas prom, but Grandpa was proud all over again that we had it to wear. Now, years later, I have the mink in a box stored at my house. Sometimes I take it out, admire its beauty, and rub my hands on the soft fur.

At Christmas, when memories flood back on the sounds of carols, the smell of pine, and the sight of red velvet bows, I remember the joy in Grandpa's eyes, that he could provide such an opulent gift. I also remember the pain of disappointment in Gran's eyes, that it was not what she really wanted, and her generous acceptance of the gift with no complaint.

It was the true Christmas spirit of giving and receiving and, as a child in the midst of that particular season, that one exchange taught me so much. Grandpa gave his best, and Gran graciously received it.

Window Shopping

BY CONNIE VIGIL PLATT

Christmas during the Great Depression resulted in few store-bought items beneath my tree. But at the age of six, all I recall was that my parents and a favorite uncle made my holiday special. They brought in a huge log for the fireplace, and we sang carols around the piano while my mother played. And to be sure Santa could get down the chimney after we had gone to bed, the adults stayed up and waited.

Shortly after midnight, my father woke us from our sound sleep and told us Santa Claus had come and gone already! We hurried from our beds and marveled at the presents that had mysteriously appeared.

"Did you see him?" I asked anxiously.

"No, I didn't see him," Dad answered. Then he explained that he'd gone to the kitchen for a cup of coffee and when he came back, everything was already there.

Earlier that year, I had spotted a pair of boots in a store window and fallen in love. They were the most beautiful boots I'd ever seen! Though we didn't have money to buy anything, my sister and I had gotten window shopping down to a fine art. I could imagine how those boots would look and feel on my feet. I wanted those boots; I didn't care what color they were as long as they were cowboy boots—but black would be nice. Because I knew money was in short supply at our house, I also knew those boots were something only Santa Claus could bring me. I went home and wrote the necessary letter, sending it up the chimney in smoke, hoping the great man would get it in time.

For the next month, I tried my best to be a good obedient child. It seemed as if everything was against me. I was late getting home from school. I lost my book. I even forgot to feed the dog!

That Christmas, when I was handed my last present, I hoped with all my heart that Santa had gotten my letter. I un-wrapped the box in my lap carefully, doing my best to save the paper so we could use it again next year. My heart skipped a beat: There was a picture of a pair of boots on the lid. But I knew enough not to get my hopes up yet—boxes were also saved from year to year.

But when I opened the box, there they were: shiny black cowboy boots! I was so excited I almost dropped the box. Grabbing a pair of new socks, I tried to pull the boots on. But try as I may, I couldn't get them past my instep!

They were perfect . . . except they were at least one size too small. There was no way they could be returned—even I knew that. Swallowing hard, I refused to let tears of frustration fall.

"Didn't you tell Santa what size you wore?" my mother asked.

"I guess not," I replied softly.

Dad took the boots from me and rubbed oil on them until the leather became soft and pliable. Then mother found a pair of thinner socks and helped me pull the boots on. I was ecstatic! I strutted around the house the rest of the night with aching feet. I didn't care; I had my boots! And I knew Santa had brought them, too, because I knew my parents didn't have the money to buy them.

When I woke the next morning, I clomped into the kitchen with my boots on. They were still tight, but were slowly adjusting to my feet.

Mother laughed when she spotted me. "Did you sleep in them?"

"No," I answered proudly, "I got them on by myself."

I wore those boots until there was nothing left but strings of leather.

By today's standards, my family had been poor. But that Christmas I was the richest child in the world. I received not one, but two of the most wonderful gifts a child could ever ask for. Not only did I get the boots I adored, but I learned—without a doubt—that there really is a Santa Claus, too!

Wishing for Miracles

BY MARCIA E. BROWN

"**A**ll I want for Christmas is a new, bright-blue Schwinn girl's bike!"

That was my wish, plea, and mantra for more than a year.

For the three years since I had learned how to ride a bicycle in 1940, my wheels had been serviceable, but that's where it ended. They got me around, yes, but they were an embarrassment to me, for they were attached to a very old, rusty boy's bike that my Dad had bought for five dollars at a police auction.

It had not been easy to learn to ride a bicycle so large that my short legs could not reach both pedals at the same time. Even at the age of twelve, I was unable to brake with both feet. My method of halting was to try to swing one leg over the high bar that made it a boy's bike and jump off as the bike slowed down, which didn't always work on the hills in my hometown, and scraped knees were a constant badge of thwarted effort.

As I moved into the sensitive teen years, my girlfriends all had girl's bikes, which they gracefully mounted and dismounted. They could also wear skirts to ride. Pleated skirts, white blouses, saddle oxfords, and bobby socks were the uniform of the day, not casual pants. A new feminine-designed bike became a serious issue for me.

My dream was to own a bright-blue girl's Schwinn. But at that time, companies like Schwinn were geared to "war production." They were permitted by the Federal Government to manufacture only a limited number of bicycles during each year of World War II, and long waiting lists soon formed. How many were allotted to northwest Arkansas dealers I have been unable to learn, but I know from experience it was mighty few. Between wartime shortage and the lack of parental funds for such a luxury, it did not look as if my wish would be granted anytime soon.

A year passed. Christmas came and went and I was still peddling the old boy's bike.

As another Christmas approached—1943—my longing for a girl's bike remained strong. But it was tinged with realism. I no longer believed in Santa Claus, and I knew that all over the country thousands of youngsters were wishing for new bicycles. For me to wish was to wish for a miracle.

On Christmas Eve, heavy snow fell on Fort Smith. It was not unusual that Dad, a newspaperman, did not come home until well after I was in bed. I woke on Christmas morning feeling sad. Because of gas rationing and Dad's work schedule, we were not going to my grandparent's for our usual joyful time with extended family, either. Snow and sleet from the night before had left our town at the southern end of the Ozarks Mountains covered with snow and ice. I lay in bed a long time, expecting a less-than-wonderful Christmas.

When at last I stepped from my unheated back bedroom into the living room, I came into brilliant morning sunshine sparkling on the blue metal of a brand new girl's Schwinn bicycle parked next to our small Christmas tree!

Miracle of miracles! It was the bicycle of my dreams. A red bow was tied to the large metal basket in front of wide chrome handlebars. A headlight for night riding rested above the blue and white front fender. Behind the comfortable seat was a passenger seat with springs for holding school books. There was even a bell on the handlebar. It was the Cadillac of bicycles for a young girl! At last I, too, could cycle to school wearing a pleated skirt, just like my friends.

Unknown to me, however, my grandfather had submitted his name along with a deposit to a Fort Smith bicycle dealer more than sixteen months earlier. My father—who had not been working late—had, in fact, walked the bike home five miles through sleet and snow on Christmas Eve, and my mother had stayed up later still to dry and polish every inch of chrome and painted metal. To this day, it brings tears to my eyes when I think back and realize, unbeknownst to me, my entire family had been wishing for a miracle, too, that Christmas. And the miracle they unselfishly sought was for me.

The Perfect Gift

BY HELEN LUECKE

Babs, my older sister, and I sat on the plane and stared out into the fluffy white clouds. I tried unsuccessfully to shut out the happy festive sounds of the people around us.

"Cozy, are you okay?" Babs asked. I nodded, not speaking.

"Merry Christmas," the flight attendant said, as she passed out refreshments. She flipped her head so everyone could see the cute red-and-green elf cap she wore. Laughter filled the plane. I wiped my eyes with the soggy tissue and leaned back against the seat. It was December 23, 1973, a few days before Christmas, but I wasn't happy. Babs and I were on our way home to see our father for the last time.

Sandra, our younger sister, was waiting for us when the plane landed. Once we were settled in the car, we began the short drive to Memphis, Texas.

"How's Momma?" I asked.

"She's doing good, but it bothers her because Daddy doesn't know her. He won't recognize ya'll either," Sandra said sadly.

"Do the doctors still say it's hardening of the arteries?" Babs asked.

Sandra nodded, "The past year he has really gone down. The last couple of months he hasn't been able to get out of bed. Remember how he used to get on his knees and pray the sweetest prayers? Now he doesn't know what a prayer is."

We drove in silence. Memories of Daddy flooded my mind. "Remember when he bought us a bicycle and taught us how to ride it?" Laughter filled the car. Babs and Sandra joined in with, "Remember the softball games, the fishing trips, his vegetable gardens, and how he taught us to skate?" All the kids in the neighborhood loved to come over to our house and play because Shack, Daddy's nickname for Shackelford, which was his real name, would come out and play with us.

By the time we arrived home, we were laughing so hard about Daddy teaching us to drive we had to catch our breath.

"He should have a gold medal for that accomplishment," Babs said.

We pulled up in front of the old familiar house and went in. Momma met us at the door with a hug. A green fir Christmas tree sat in the corner with flashing lights and sparkling decorations; the smell of fried chicken, biscuits, gravy, and peach cobbler filled the room; and a blast of nostalgia encircled me. I wanted to run and jump into my daddy's strong arms and feel him swing me around. I closed my eyes and let the moment pass.

I wasn't prepared for the change. His small, firm, wiry body was thin and bony.

I kissed his sunken cheek and whispered, "Hi, Daddy, I love you."

When there was no response, no recognition whatsoever, I turned and hurried into the kitchen. Babs, Sandra, and Momma soon followed. We sat at the table, loaded with our favorite meal, with no appetites. The family of our childhood was around the table, but one important member was missing.

Finally, Momma said, "Let's take our coffee and cobbler into the living room."

We made small talk about the weather, the Christmas tree, and our flight, then Momma took over the conversation and got down to business.

"The doctor said Shack could live a month, two at the most. He can't get out of bed, he doesn't know anyone, and he doesn't eat much."

I took a bite of peach cobbler as Momma continued, "You know that your daddy is a Christian. He's ready to go home to be with Jesus." She took a sip of coffee and added, "The next two days, visit with Shack, talk with him, sing, and enjoy this special time that God has given us to be with him."

The next morning, I went into Daddy's room. He sat propped up in bed. I climbed up beside him and took his frail hand. I looked into his pale blue eyes.

"Daddy, I'll never forget the basketball you gave me for Christmas when I was in the sixth grade. I bounced that ball until it was threadbare. Because of you and that ball, I became a better player. I think that was the best gift ever."

Daddy squeezed my hand, and for a minute, I thought he remembered the ball and understood what I had said. Then he asked, softly, "Do you know the woman who takes care of me?"

I nearly cried. "That's your wife. She takes good care of you. She loves you. We all do," I whispered.

I stayed in his room for several hours talking, singing, combing his hair, and rubbing lotion on his arms. Babs and Sandra visited with him the rest of the day while Momma— determined this would be a good Christmas for the whole family—stayed busy in the kitchen cooking turkey and dressing and baking pies and cakes for Christmas Day.

Later that evening, Sandra's family came up to join us for Christmas Eve gifts. We included Daddy in everything. When we sang "Silent Night" and "Away in a Manger," he smiled and nodded. Then we gave him his presents: pajamas, fuzzy socks, and a blue house coat.

We kissed him goodnight, then went into the kitchen to help Momma get things ready for Christmas dinner. That night in bed, I thought of the good time I had spent with Daddy, and I knew I had only one more day before I would have to leave. Then it would be goodbye—maybe forever.

"Lord," I prayed, "If it be Your will, let Daddy recognize me just once. Let me see his blue eyes sparkle with that *Hi, Cozy, I love you* look. Amen."

Christmas Day dawned cloudy and gray, with huge silent snowflakes drifting down. During the morning, the preacher and several members from the church stopped by to see Daddy, and Aunt Mae came by with banana pudding and rolls. At noon, we brought Christmas dinner in to Daddy and sat with him. He ate some mashed potatoes, a small portion of white turkey, and some banana pudding. After a while he dozed off, so we went into the living room.

I was curled up on the couch, ready for a nap, when we heard a noise in Daddy's room. Afraid he had fallen out of bed, we rushed to his room. Daddy was kneeling beside his bed, his head bowed, his hands folded. His weak voice was now strong as he gave praise, glory, and love to the Lord. We listened with tears streaming down our faces. Minutes later, he stood and climbed back into bed.

Because of Daddy's deep faith, God had given him—and us—the perfect Christmas gift: the strength to say his last prayer the way he always had—on bended knees.

The Truth about Santa

by Bridget Balthrop Morton

I discovered the truth about Santa the year I turned nine. My family had spent the summer in a small house on Pensacola Bay, swimming on the beach or getting lost in the backwoods, then falling asleep to the lullaby of waves. We loved our old house on the water, even though the house had only two bedrooms and we were a family of six children.

Like an army on the march, we kept trying new sleeping plans. Should all the girls sleep in one bedroom, with the boys on the porch, and our parents in the large master bedroom? Or, should the parents move to the living room so the boys could have the bedroom and the girls could go in the big room? We tried these plans and more. Nobody expected privacy. My mother occasionally sighed that she had no place to sew, not that she had time for it anyway. We dreamed that one day we'd know which bed was really ours.

The year before, Santa had brought me a Madame Alexander doll, with dark curls around a smiling face. She looked nothing like me, and I adored her. I played with my dolls, unlike my sister Mary. Her much grander Queen Victoria doll remained perched primly, in her gold brocade, on a dresser in whichever room we slept. Mary forbade us to touch her, and so she remained what she had been: a beautiful doll, untouched and unsoiled. I brushed my doll's hair till her curls were matted, her sweet face as dirty as my own. We tramped through the same puddles to bake mud pies, and if I remembered to wash my face, I scrubbed hers with the same washcloth.

Need I say my doll was naked? I can't even remember her original clothes. My doll and I didn't bother much with clothes, but Mother insisted that I at least had to wear them.

I still have that doll in the back of my closet, though I can't remember her name. Maybe, like my sleeping arrangements, I renamed her on a daily basis. I know for certain she had more than one personality. Some days, she was better than I would ever be, and far, far worse on others. But she always understood me perfectly.

That fall, her nakedness began to bother me, so I asked Santa to bring her a ball gown. I even remember my letter. I wrote that the color didn't matter, as long as the evening gown sparkled. The details I left to Santa.

I waited distractedly for Christmas. I remembered Santa liked bright red. I did not, and I doubted my doll did, either. I had not asked for anything else.

On Christmas Eve, our parents delivered their annual bedtime directives. No one was allowed out of bed before dawn or to enter the living room alone. We would all go in together, as always. We children, bouncy and nervous, nodded. Only recently have we shared our memories of breaking those rules.

That Christmas Eve when I woke, my parents had already returned from Midnight Mass. When I moved slightly, I saw Christmas lights reflected in the windows. Gradually, I heard the comforting sounds of my family sleeping and climbed down from the top bunk bed. I stared at my sister in the lower bunk and struggled with my conscience. The living room was so close. No one would ever know.

The Christmas tree shimmered in impossible quiet. I refused to look in the corner where my name was placed—the spot where my gifts would be. I knew precisely what my siblings had asked for, and I padded reverently from name to name. Santa had provided the secret wish of every child in my family, a gift each had really wanted. I wondered how he did it.

I was still afraid to look for my doll's dress.

Finally, more afraid of being discovered than of what I might see, I turned toward the corner where my gift should be. There was my doll, where I'd left her to wait for her new gown. She wore a white satin dress with a fitted bodice and a princess skirt. The white tulle overlay was awash with gold glitter. The dress twinkled as brightly as the tree. I reached out but I did not touch. I had never seen such a beautiful dress.

Something glimmered in the corner of my eye. A sky-blue evening gown hung nearby. I caught my breath and held it. The dress looked exactly my size, but I would have to wait until morning to be sure. This dress was simpler than my doll's, but floor length, and the skirt was studded with diamonds. When I closed my eyes and imagined heaven, it looked like that dress.

I crept back to bed more mystified than before. I had not known I wanted that dress until I saw it. But now that I had seen it, I could think of little else. Pondering this, I drifted back to sleep.

In the morning, the dress fit as if it had been tailored for me.

However had Santa done it? I asked over and over.

My brother, against every rule, dribbled his new basketball into the house. He stopped beside me, nearly growling at my continued question.

"When will you learn?" he asked, stupefied at my ignorance. "Santa knows everything!"

The Saint and the Santa

BY ANNEMARIEKE TAZELAAR

When my father pulled our 1939 black Ford sedan into the Chicago intersection of Lake Shore Drive and Jackson Boulevard to make a left turn, a policeman blew his whistle, held out his hand to stop traffic, and approached the car.

"What in the Sam Hill?" Papa said under his breath. He rolled down the window cautiously, wondering what he'd done wrong.

The officer extended his hand and asked, "Where are you heading?" Then he peered into the car, his eyes stopping on my mother. I watched her profile as she smiled at him, an earring dangling beneath the lace cap of her Dutch costume. From the back seat, I saw my father's shoulders relax. The officer was merely curious.

"The Museum of Science and Industry," Papa answered. "My family is supposed to be on stage in two hours."

The policeman scanned my two siblings and me, costumed and shy, sitting stone still in the back seat. "Where are you folks from?" he asked.

"Grand Rapids," Papa said.

"The Netherlands," Mama offered, leaning over my father to look up at the officer. "We came here less than a year ago."

"No kidding? You folks must've been in the war!"

My father's eyes answered the police officer's question silently. Sometimes, when talking about the war, there was too much to say, sometimes there was nothing to say. Sometimes, we were just glad we had lived through it all, and yet sometimes—like right now—I could think of some very fond memories that could never have taken place if there hadn't been a war.

Taking the hint, the officer quickly changed the subject. After explaining the most direct way to the museum, he wished us good luck on stage and waved us on.

A college friend of my father's had arranged for our participation in the 1946 Christmas Around the World program at the museum. On our way to the auditorium, we clomped on our wooden shoes through a long hallway lined with Christmas trees decked out in the traditions of many countries.

Dazzled by the grandeur of the lights, the decorations, and the huge trees, my mind wandered back to another Christmas, two years before, in war-torn Arnhem—our beloved city. We were evacuated, so our family and my mother's parents had rented two rooms in a nearby village. For Christmas that year, the seven of us shared one small chicken, garnished with potatoes and rutabagas gleaned from the fields, and fresh mushrooms found in the forest: a feast, compared to our usual meager fare of boiled potatoes.

And we had a tree. My father cut three pine branches, tied them together, and "planted" them in a bucket of soil. The amorphous shape kept flopping over until we leaned the tree against a wall.

My brothers and I took charge of decorating the "tree." From colored scraps of paper, we fashioned five-pointed stars and nativity scene characters, which we cut out and hung on twigs. On the forest floor, we found silver strips—radio distorters dropped from British planes to thwart German communications. These we draped on the branches. The bright tinsel sparkled as candlelight transformed our ugly duckling tree into a Christmas swan.

That was then. Now, we were scheduled to enact the traditional Dutch St. Nicholas celebration. Although we had never worn costumes in the Netherlands, the museum staff wanted us to don them, so Mother had hastily cobbled our outfits together. I felt proud and pretty in my lace cap and long skirt. My brothers grinned sheepishly when they tried on their wide, billowing breeches. We all needed practice walking in wooden shoes.

Someone led Mother and my brothers and me to a stage furnished with a living room façade: a wall with a single door and pictures of windmills and tulips. A decorated tree stood to one side. Mother tried to explain to the stage director that the December 5th St. Nicholas celebration and Christmas had nothing to do with one another, but the Christmas theme won over authenticity, so the tree stayed.

Mother tested the upright piano with a few chords and arpeggios. Satisfied, she rehearsed a song with us before the doors of the huge auditorium opened. *But where was my father?*

Backstage sat a dozen or so "wooden shoe" dancers—girls from Holland, Michigan. A short, stocky man held the reins of a white horse, which looked somewhat nervous, and doing what horses tend to do any time they feel the urge, the horse suddenly let go with an impressive splash that bounced off the wooden floor and onto the bevy of girls. The girls jumped up, screamed, and scattered.

With a booming voice, their coach soothed them. "Ladies, please settle down! It'll dry!"

We watched the worried horse owner trying to calm the animal as a stagehand appeared with a bucket and a mop. We peeked out from behind the side curtain at the gathering audience, a huge mass of people to our apprehensive eyes. Suddenly, the street-organ dance music began and the girls filed out, now quite composed and self-confident. The performance ended and the applause cascaded with thunderous appreciation. The curtain came down, and we took our place on the stage.

Mother opened the St. Nicholas songbook to a favorite we all knew by heart, about the moon shining through the trees and St. Nicholas, astride his white steed, riding from rooftop to rooftop. When the curtain rose again, we were already singing.

The door of the backdrop opened, and a black-gloved hand tossed candy onto the carpet. We scrambled for the sweets, singing the traditional song that accompanied the action.

Then the door opened again. The white steed we'd seen back stage entered. Astride sat St. Nicholas in a white robe, a gold stole, and a tall mitered hat. St. Nicholas would have looked quite regal, except that the animal balked, its eyes growing big and round. And St. Nicholas, awkward in the saddle, certainly didn't look as though he could handle a whole evening of rooftop riding!

Nodding to the good Saint, my mother played the introduction to "Welcome to Our House, Honored Bishop," as my older brother and I sang.

But not my younger brother, Hans. He stood, openmouthed, looking at his beloved St. Nicholas. The audience fell silent, and my mother stopped playing to see what had captured their attention. We all stared at Hans.

Then, with a gasp, totally oblivious to his surroundings, Hans blurted out, "That's Papa!"

Laughter exploded from the audience. Then the applause thundered, realizing they had witnessed a rite of passage for my brother: his entry into the adult world of realism. His childhood idol was, after all, merely mortal.

At the reception that followed our performance, a sea of people milled around us, smiling, murmuring appreciation for our skit, complimenting our costumes and our voices. We gravitated toward a table laden with platters of turkey, mashed potatoes, salads, and pies.

"All that food!" my mother exclaimed, choking back tears.

And then, we heard a jingle of bells and a booming voice that filled the room. The crowd parted to make way for a corpulent Santa Claus walking toward my tall, lanky father, who was still dressed in his bishop garments.

We watched every move of the jolly man with the magnificent white beard. Santa opened a large bag and held up a candy cane for Hans.

Then, a smiling Saint and a smiling Santa shook hands. A glimmer of wonder returned to my brother's eyes. And as two traditions mingled, a young boy's faith was restored.

A Musical Miracle

BY AL SERRADELL

My family has always been a great collector of people. Mom was especially gifted in this sport, so gifted, in fact, that I never knew whom she'd bring home for dinner or a holiday celebration. Her strategy was simple: If she met someone she thought needed comforting or just companionship, within twenty-four hours her new friend would be sitting at our table enjoying a home-cooked meal. I remember one Christmas holiday in particular, when I came home from college to find a strange woman sitting in our living room. She wore a shapeless denim smock and looked to be about forty-something. With no makeup, her hair tied in a long graying ponytail, she appeared haggard and worn, a living portrait of a rough life.

After a quick hug, my mother introduced me to her new best friend.

"Say hello to Grace, Al. She's visiting us from St. Grace," Mom added.

St. Grace was a local nursing home. Images of old, bedridden people too feeble to move flooded my brain. But surely something was wrong. Grace didn't appear to be old and looked pretty healthy, at least strong enough to feed herself.

I smiled and said hello to our visitor. Instead of responding, the strange woman sat perfectly still, her gaze fixed forward, not even looking at me. I wasn't sure she'd even heard me, so I said hello again, louder this time.

Still nothing.

Mom bridged the awkward silence with small talk, which she continued throughout dinner, informing us that our visitor had no blood family to speak of and so was anxious to make new friends. Knowing our mother's strict rules on hospitality, we tried conversing with our guest. "Don't you love Christmas?" "I haven't even had a chance to do much shopping." "What's your favorite Christmas carol?" On and on we went, ignoring her silence while refilling her plate and water glass every few minutes.

After dinner, one of my brothers decided to hook up the karaoke machine. I wasn't sure this was such a good idea. Grace wasn't having a very good time as it was. Sitting like a statue, not saying a word, she was probably counting the minutes until she could return to the peace and quiet of her own room. But the family tradition won out, as each of us started going through the offered selections to choose our musical numbers. When the songbook was passed to Grace, she just nodded and said, "Number 135."

I checked the list. Patsy Cline. "Crazy."

Uh-oh, I thought. *This is it.* The theme song for the infirmed—Grace was about to crack. I wondered if we'd have to call an ambulance to take her back to the nursing home or a mental ward. After all, she hadn't uttered a sound since her arrival here—surely this would only push her over the edge. But my worries proved groundless. When her turn came, I was shocked. Not only could Grace vocalize, but she sang well—soft and slow, with perfect phrasing and pitch and without even looking at the words on the monitor. She knew the song, and had no doubt performed it before!

Afterward, we applauded and Mom handed our guest the songbook again. This time, the woman chose a Christmas song.

Closing her eyes, Grace poured every ounce of emotion and power into her performance, as if she were onstage. I could feel the song coming to life for her, the joy of Christmas rising from her soul.

I felt the trickle of tears rolling down my face. Grace had blown me away. Looking around, I realized she'd achieved the same effect on everyone in the room. Never had we enjoyed a more beautiful and emotional rendition of "Silent Night."

Wanting to know how she had learned to sing that well, I risked a conversation with our singing guest.

A smile lit up her face. "Honey," Grace said in a hoarse, whispery tone, "I sang in a band with my husband for nearly fifteen years. We weren't really professional, but folks seemed to enjoy our singing of the popular songs." She stopped for a minute, and I thought she was finished for the night, but after a moment she continued. "When Sammy died, I just stopped singing. It was like I just didn't have the heart anymore. But tonight, with all of you around, I thought I could try it again."

I put my arm around her. "Well, you can come sing for us anytime."

"For fifteen years I sang with that man," she explained. "Fifteen wonderful years."

Grace's eyes sparkled, and I knew she was thinking of Sammy and singing in their band. All those memories had come back, and she was happy once again. I looked at Mom and a feeling of pride raced through me. Not everyone would invite a stranger into their home, but because Mom had, Grace had come out of mourning and was enjoying the warmth of just plain being alive again.

The Last Apple

BY DMITRI BARVINOK

In Slonim, Belarussia, the holidays are celebrated by giving what we can to the needy. That same sense of gift giving circulates down through homes and businesses. Even the day care my little brother, Nicholas, attended always hosted a large celebration, complete with a huge Christmas tree, lots of fruit punch, and presents.

The families of those who attend the day care always come for a bit of holiday cheer, bringing friends and relatives with them. One year, the celebration at the day care was particularly large. At the age of six, my best friend, Kiriil, and I couldn't wait for everyone to arrive so we could grab a piece of fruit or a cookie! As soon as we were given the go ahead, Kiriil selected an apple from the table and shoved it into his pocket, while I grabbed a few cookies for us to share in the big room where the festivities were to take place.

We children looked forward to this event and couldn't wait to check out the tree! The Christmas tree stretched up to the ceiling and was draped with shiny ornaments, presents, and candy!

Soon, we were standing beneath the tree looking at the huge assortment of gifts—including a brightly knitted pair of mittens—with a simple tag that read: To ANTON C. FOR A FENCE WELL PAINTED.

As we crowded around the tree, adults took various presents off the branches or from under the tree, read the inscription, and passed the gifts on to the prospective recipient. Kiriil and I waited patiently while lucky children raced back to their parents shouting, "Look what I got!"

Grandparents smiled at the chaos, nodding with glistening eyes as they watched the expression on each child's face.

Every year, for as long as I could remember, we always returned home pleased with the new toys we received. It was always an evening filled with happiness from beginning to end. No one expected this year would be different. But in the midst of the holiday happiness, someone rushed into the room shouting that a fire had broken out in the kitchen, and mass chaos ensued!

For a moment, Kiriil and I froze. Then we heard parents yelling for their children, children screaming for their parents. The unmistakable smell of smoke wafted through the doors from the kitchen, and almost immediately, a grey-black cloud rolled into the main room. As people started coughing, those closest to the emergency exit finally got it open and the fire alarm shrieked, adding to the din. Strong arms grabbed us and helped us outside, where we stood for the next few minutes, watching the commotion with wide eyes and wondering where our families were.

Though the excitement of the Christmas Party had taken a frightening turn, even at our young age we could see that in the midst of the horror, goodness had taken over. Those with cell phones dialed 911, while others ran for fire extinguishers. Adults grabbed youngsters—including both of our younger siblings—and hauled them safely from the burning building, and teenagers helped the elderly.

Soon, everyone had congregated outside. As flames lit the night sky, parents counted their children to make sure no one had been left behind. When we heard the first fire siren, a collective sigh of relief fanned through the group. Many looked up at the night sky—some to our Creator, some just to the beauty of the stars. For the first time ever, I realized how precious my vision was, something I had taken for granted before today.

Bonded by trauma, Kiriil's family clumped together with ours as we made our way home.

The next week, as other organizations celebrated the holidays, the day care director posted a small note on a local bulletin board asking for donations to help rebuild the center. Then she placed a small box beneath the note.

When Kiriil and his younger sister, Tanya, accompanied by their grandmother, saw the request and the empty box, Kiriil turned to his grandmother.

"Grandma," he said, "I want to talk to the lady in charge of the day care. I have an apple that I kept from the party." The old woman smiled. Moved by her brother's kindness, Tanya smiled, too. She pulled a dollar bill from her pocket and asked if she could donate it to the cause as well.

The woman beamed with pride as she took her grandchildren to see the director. When the story spread throughout the area, the community came alive with the Spirit of Christmas, and donations began to pour in!

The director was so touched by Kiriil's gesture that she, too, made a gesture. She announced that anyone who donated to the fund would get a small slice of the apple as a symbolic gesture of her thankfulness and appreciation.

Over the next month, there were so many donations offered, there was no way an apple could be divided into that many pieces. To make up for it, the director mailed a small plastic replica of an apple—the sort teachers might keep on their desks—to each contributor, with a small plaque bearing the words "To Those Who Care and Give." And, to mark the generosity of a child, the director decided to add a new tradition to the festivities.

When Christmas came the following year, the day care director retold the story of what had happened the previous Christmas. After she finished praising the community for their quick thinking during a time of panic, she told a story about a little boy who had donated his apple—all that he had to give—in hopes it would help the rebuilding of the center. Then, she asked Kiriil to step forward to accept not only a generous round of applause, but also the first apple of the evening.

Though it's been a dozen years since that Christmas, this tradition still continues, in honor of Kiriil, the "best" best friend I've ever had the pleasure of knowing.

Forty Dollars

BY DONNA SUNDBLAD

Large snowflakes drifted past the window while my husband poured over our finances. Two years ago, a failed business had buried us in debt, but by following a budget, we were gradually digging our way out.

Rick rubbed his eyes. "Well," he said as he leaned back in his chair and stretched, "we have forty dollars for Christmas." He shrugged. "It's better than nothing."

I glanced out the window. *Forty dollars*. Our children needed winter boots, coats—they'd done without necessities for so long. How would I explain, once again, that they would have to do without?

I shouldn't have worried. Our eleven-year old and nine-year-old children accepted the disappointment like battle-weary troopers.

A couple of days later, my youngest sister called from Florida. With thirteen years between us, my relationship with her had taken on the role of second mother. At seventeen, she desperately wanted to come home for Christmas.

"I'll see what we can do," I promised.

As the eldest of seven siblings, I hoped we could work together to make this a reality. I knew none of us had the resources to get her home alone. I checked airfare and then divided the cost equally. I blinked at the calculator readout: Forty dollars.

Later, I explained to each sibling, "If we each chip in forty dollars . . . " After the last call, I slumped in my chair. I pondered the consequences for a few minutes, and then laid out the scenario for our kids. They didn't hesitate. My sister—their aunt—was coming home for Christmas.

Their unselfishness touched my heart, yet my spirit grieved. The following day, I shared my mixed emotions with the nurse at the school where I worked. She encouraged me to be proud of my children. That wasn't the problem. I couldn't be prouder, but they deserved better.

Later that week, I poured out my concerns with my prayer group. Tears trickled and embarrassment burned my cheeks. Everyone gathered around to thank God for the kids' unselfishness, and to ask God to bless them.

At home, we set up our tree and placed a "thankfulness box" beneath it. In the days leading to Christmas, family members wrote what they were thankful for on slips of paper. The notes were then dropped into the box to be read on Christmas morning as our gifts to one another.

Two days later, while I sat in the break room at work, one of the teachers handed me a Christmas card. Because every goodwill gesture hurt as much as it brought pleasure, my emotions clashed as I opened the card with a stoic smile. The generic Christmas wishes on the card said little, but I stared in shock at the crisp one-hundred-dollar bill tucked inside.

"This . . . " I cleared my emotion-choked throat. "This is an answer to prayer." I looked around the room to see smiles on faces of teachers and staff now gathering around me. "You don't know what this means," I said. "The kids will be so surprised."

With Christmas only a week away, my mind raced with possibilities. We'd have presents under the tree after all! If I was careful and shopped the sales, our children would have new coats and boots and maybe—just maybe—something fun.

That Wednesday, when my family attended Bible study and prayer, I prayed with a new thankfulness. I couldn't wait to share how God had answered my prayer from the week before. Plus, my sister would arrive in two days! It couldn't get much better than this.

After the meeting concluded, people gathered in small clusters wishing each other Merry Christmas. Mrs. Casper wrapped her arms around me in a warm hug and handed me a gaily wrapped box. This hard-working, middle-aged woman told me she had made cookies for our family, and not to leave the package until Christmas morning to open or the cookies would be stale.

I thanked her for her kindness and planned to add another "thank you" to the box under the tree at home.

When we located the kids in the fellowship hall, they eyed the gift in my hands with unspoken wonder. I blinked back tears as I realized how surprised they would be Christmas morning.

"It's from Mrs. Casper," I said. "She made cookies for us."

We scurried across the cold, almost empty, dimly lit parking lot to the car—the lake-effect wind biting through our winter coats. My husband and I slipped into the front seat and slammed the doors against the wind. The back doors opened, but the kids stood there, letting the wind whip through the car.

"Hurry up and get in," I said.

"There're bags back here," my son said.

"Grocery bags," my daughter added.

My husband and I exchanged a glance and climbed from the car.

"Oranges!" Heather said as she dug through the bags. "And a turkey!"

The paper bags held all the fixings for a Christmas dinner and more! Christmas tunes on the car radio added the perfect touch on the ride home. We each walked into the house carrying a bag, and talked excitedly while putting the groceries away. After we were finished, the kids added a special thank you to the thankfulness box for yet another secret Santa.

"When you're done, get ready for bed and we'll have a few cookies," I said as I ripped the gift wrap from the box and opened the lid. They glanced at the variety of sweets and rushed upstairs to change.

I pulled the card from the box, handed it to my husband, and put the tea kettle on. Such a special night called for hot chocolate.

"I can't believe it," he said as he pressed his finger to his lips and held the card at an angle for me to see the check.

Two hundred and fifty dollars! This hardworking farming family had given us two hundred and fifty dollars!

The next evening, I went shopping while the children thought I'd gone to help my mother decorate Christmas cookies. Walking through the store with money to spend seemed more dream than reality. Tears threatened each time I placed an item in my cart. My sister was coming home, we had three hundred and fifty dollars to spend, *and* we had enough groceries to make a fine Christmas dinner.

My family has never been more thankful than we were that Christmas morning, when we read the notes in our thankfulness box and wrote heartfelt thank-you cards to all of the generous people in our life.

Memories of a Refugee Camp Christmas

BY RENIE BURGHARDT

During World War II, we had many sad Christmases. Fear always lurked in some nearby corner. During those times we observed Christmas mainly in our hearts. So, in 1947 when we arrived in the refugee camp in Austria just a few weeks before Christmas, I wasn't expecting anything different. At the age of eleven, I had become resigned to not having much.

The refugee camp, with its wooden barracks and dusty lanes, was pretty drab. But we had a place to sleep, food to eat, and were outfitted with warm clothes, donated to the refugee effort from various generous-minded countries like the United States, Canada, and Great Britain. We considered ourselves pretty fortunate. To top it off, since the camp was located in Carinthia, one of the most scenic areas of Austria, we had some of the most beautiful views available.

As Christmas approached, the refugee camp school I attended made plans to help us celebrate the holiday as a group. In the barracks we lived in, our private sleeping spaces were tiny cubicles with no room for individual celebrations, but the school had a large auditorium where a donated Christmas tree was set up, which we children had helped decorate with our own handmade ornaments. There were candles on the tree, too, which were to be lit Christmas Eve, just like it used to be done in Hungary before the war. Additionally, we were rehearsing the school Christmas play, to be presented on Christmas Eve. I had a small part in the play, as the angel who comes to give the message to the shepherds about the birth of the Savior, and was very pleased and excited about the part.

On the afternoon of Christmas Eve, my grandparents and I decided to take a walk to the small town of Spittal, a few miles from camp. Grandfather felt that even though we had no money to buy anything, taking in the Christmas sights and smells would be worth the walk. The town's cobbled streets, with its many small shops, were decorated with fir branches, and small trees in shop windows glowed with lit candles. People hustled and bustled, getting last-minute items for the holiday, and wishing each other "Froliche Weinachten!"

We stopped in front of the bakery and inhaled the delicious smells coming from the door every time someone opened it. I gazed at the Napoleons in the window, my mouth watering.

"Oh, they must taste so delicious," I said wistfully.

"And that poppy seed kalacs (kuchen) looks wonderful, too," Grandmother sighed.

"Maybe this wasn't such a good idea," Grandfather said. "Now everyone is hungry for something they cannot have."

"But who is to say that you cannot have a Napoleon, or some of that poppy seed kuchen?" a voice behind us asked, as a woman in a fur coat and hat took my hand. "Come on! Let us all go into the bakery."

"Oh, no!" I protested, trying to pull my hand from her grip. But she wouldn't take no for an answer. Inside the bakery, she bought a large Napoleon square and some kuchen, just for us!

"Froliche Weinachten!" she called merrily as she disappeared into a crowd of people.

I gazed in awe at her retreating form, my mind forming one thought: *I had been visited by a Christmas angel in a fur coat!*

As I sunk my teeth into that delicious custard-filled Napoleon on the way back to the refugee camp, powdered sugar spilled down my face and chest. I hugged myself in delight. I was already so happy this Christmas, and I knew there were more wonderful surprises ahead!

On Christmas Eve, the candles on the community Christmas tree were lit and all the adults in camp came to watch our Christmas play. Everyone remembered their lines, and the choir sang beautiful Hungarian Christmas songs. We all had tears in our eyes by the time they were finished. Then each child was given one present.

When I opened mine, I found a pair of fuzzy red mittens and a matching scarf. Inside one of the mittens, there was a little note, written in English, that read: MERRY CHRISTMAS FROM MARY ANNE, IN BUFFALO, NEW YORK, UNITED STATES OF AMERICA. I was stunned to receive a gift from a girl all the way in America!

When I awoke on Christmas morning, the morning sun, as well as happy noises, poured in through the thin wooden boards of the barrack.

"Good morning, sweetheart," Grandmother said. "Merry Christmas!"

"Why is there so much noise out there already?" I asked sleepily.

"Well, I guess some early rising children are enjoying all the newly fallen snow," she said calmly as a smile played about her lips.

"Snow!" I leapt from the cot and scrambled to dress. "How wonderful! And where is Grandfather?"

"He and some of the other men are shoveling paths, so people can go for their breakfast, and to church."

Within seconds, I was outside, marveling at Nature's power to turn a drab refugee camp into a pristine winter wonderland! Nature's gift was free for everyone to enjoy. It wasn't long before the surrounding snow-covered hills were filled with squealing Austrian children, enjoying the snow as much as the refugee children did.

Later, as I gazed at the majestic snow-covered mountains with their snow-dusted spruce trees—so breathtakingly beautiful—my heart filled with joy. With tears in my eyes, I thanked God for the most wonderful Christmas I had ever had, and one I knew I would never forget.

Grandpa's Love

BY STELLA WARD WHITLOCK

"Look, Grandpa!" I shouted. "No hands!" I flung my arms up and then stretched them out for balance. Thick auburn pigtails bounced below my bike helmet.

A horn blared, tires screeched, and I swerved. My bike hit the curb, flipped, and slid sideways, wheels spinning crazily. I hit the road in front of the skidding car.

Grandpa ran to kneel beside me. "Stella! Are you all right?" I lay still, eyes closed as the right front tire nudged my helmet. "Stella, honey!" Grandpa touched my face. "Can you hear me?"

I moaned, struggling to get up. "Who's pulling my hair, Grandpa?" My arms and legs worked, but I couldn't lift my head. The tire on my braids held me prisoner.

"I'll back the car off," said the driver.

"Wait!" ordered Grandpa. "You might hurt her worse."

"I'll get my scissors," said a neighbor. "We'll cut off her braids."

"No!" I protested. "Don't cut my hair! Please!"

"We won't, sweetheart," Grandpa said.

"I know!" I exclaimed. "Just push the car backwards."

When the pulling on my hair stopped, I stood up, removed my helmet, and rubbed my tingling scalp. Grandpa checked me inch by inch. A scraped elbow was my only injury.

I examined the red bicycle. "Not even scratched," I said in relief. "If I'd wrecked his bike, Chris'd never let me borrow it again."

"You're fortunate," Grandpa said. "Do you realize what could've happened?"

"Yeah, another inch and . . ." I shuddered. "Grandpa, do we have to tell Mama? If we do, she'll never get me a bike for Christmas."

"*I* won't tell her," Grandpa answered.

After a pause, I said, "I guess I'll tell her myself."

"Good girl!" Grandpa said.

When I told Mama, she didn't forbid me to ride anymore. She just talked about safety, to which I promised never to ride "no-hands" again.

As I kissed Grandpa goodnight, he gave me an extra-big hug. That was the last hug I ever got from him. His funeral was three days later.

I sat on the front pew with Mama. I felt like crying, but didn't. I hadn't cried the night the ambulance took Grandpa . . . not when Mama told me Grandpa had died . . . not when I saw him lying in his casket. And I wasn't going to cry now.

Dry-eyed, I stared straight ahead, trying not to see Grandpa lying there looking like he did every morning when I tiptoed in to kiss him goodbye before school. *Wake up, Grandpa,* I thought. *Open your eyes. Tell me you'll see me this afternoon.* A heart attack, my mother had said. But still I prayed, *Dear God, please let Grandpa wake up.*

The minister read from the Bible, but I didn't listen. How could Grandpa leave me? Did he know I loved him? Had I ever told him? The last day of his life—the day of my accident when that woman had wanted to cut my hair—Grandpa had been so reassuring. Had I thanked him then? Why hadn't I told him I loved him?

At the cemetery, the minister talked again, then took my mother's hand and murmured a few words. We drove home in silence. I felt as if I'd left my heart at the cemetery.

On Christmas Eve, I went to church with Mama. The music was beautiful, as usual. Poinsettias, candles, crèche—it was all there. All except Grandpa. I tried to swallow the lump in my throat. *Why didn't I ever tell you, Grandpa? It's too late now. Why didn't I tell you I loved you?*

I woke early on Christmas morning. The lump was still in my throat. Slowly, I pulled on my jeans and T-shirt and walked into the living room. There stood the Christmas tree, with wrapped gifts beneath it. And there stood . . . a bicycle—a shiny blue Schwinn with matching blue helmet—just what I'd always wanted. But now, somehow, it wasn't the same.

Mama stood in the doorway. "Don't you want to ride it, Stella?"

"Yeah, sure," I said listlessly. Then I noticed the white envelope on the handlebars, with my name on it in Grandpa's handwriting.

I looked at Mama, who nodded and smiled. "Open it, honey." I ripped open the envelope and read:

Dearest Stella,

I hope riding this bicycle gives you as much joy as seeing you ride gives me.

I'll always love you, Grandpa

For the first time since Grandpa died, tears came. Grandpa had gotten this bike for me before he died. He said he would always love me. And of course he knew I loved him, too. Suddenly, I felt gladness sweep over me.

I grabbed the handlebars and wheeled my shiny new bike into the daylight. I put on my helmet, jumped onto my bike, and started pedaling. I flung my arms up for a moment, then grasped the handlebars quickly.

"Look, Grandpa!" I shouted. "Two hands! Thank you! I love you, too!"

A Gift for Veronica

by Cherie Troped

At the age of thirteen, Veronica was tiny. She wore her hair pulled back in two braids, which were always neatly tied with ribbons. Every Saturday, she painfully made her way into the hospital, pausing to rest for a moment at the Information Desk where I worked as a volunteer.

My greetings to her were always rewarded with a luminous smile, as she made her way to the elevator for her kidney dialysis treatment. I noticed she was always alone.

"My grandma drops me off," she explained. "It makes her too sad to be in the hospital. You see, my momma died here last year."

Veronica and her mother shared more than just memories—they shared lupus—an autoimmune disease that literally attacks the body from within. Veronica's kidneys were badly damaged. One had been removed and the other wasn't working well enough to cleanse her body of toxins. Veronica admitted the doctors were worried about her and that she was scared. She needed to have her remaining kidney removed.

On Christmas Eve morning, I noticed her name on the Intensive Care unit of the hospital patient roster and raced up to see her. She looked even tinier in the huge hospital bed with her brightly colored ribbons spread across the pillow. Still, she managed a huge smile when she saw me.

"Well, they took my other kidney," she said. "But the doctors are looking for a new one for me." Her smile widened. "Maybe I'll get a new kidney for Christmas." Exhausted from the surgery and the pain, and the knowledge that without a new kidney her life would be even harder, Veronica succumbed to blessed sleep.

Unless they found a donor organ for her, she would be forced to have dialysis treatments for the rest of her life. I looked around the hospital room. Nothing in it spoke of the holiday season. Instead of Christmas ornaments, tinsel, and a stocking, there was only an I.V. pole.

Being Jewish, my family doesn't celebrate Christmas, but I knew something had to be done for Veronica, and done that night. It was Christmas Eve, and no matter what, this child needed a Christmas (or Chanukah) miracle.

I didn't know what to do. Because I had to remain at my desk and the hospital was short-staffed due to the holiday, I called my father and explained the situation.

"Daddy," I pleaded. "We've got to do something!"

That night, my father and mother delivered a fully decorated tree to Veronica's room as she lay asleep in her bed. I took the huge bag of presents from my mom and put them near the tree, which was beautifully but strangely decorated with a half-dozen large red Christmas ornaments.

My mother smiled at my confusion. "Your father never bought Christmas ornaments before," she said. "I guess he thought bigger was better!"

When Veronica opened her eyes the next morning, the first thing she saw was my dad, in a red sweater, standing next to the tree with presents piled high alongside it.

"Oh, Santa," she cried, "Merry Christmas." As sleep overtook her again, she whispered, "And thank you . . . Santa."

Daddy mumbled a quiet "Ho-ho-ho" and exited the room quickly.

As he told me what had happened, he wiped his eyes. "Must have gotten a cold," he muttered.

Though miracles don't always happen when you want them to, the fact that they happen at all is enough for most of us to cling to, and Veronica was no different. She finally got her new kidney, and even though it wasn't in time for Christmas, she was thrilled and happy, and best of all, healthy.

It's been years now, but I will never forget that sad little tree decorated with the huge ornaments that matched my father's generous heart, and the little girl who asked for only one thing that Christmas—a kidney.

So Little, So Much

BY JOAN FITTING SCOTT

The Coogan family was big and boisterous. With six children—five girls and one boy—there was always something going on. According to my mother, simple joys filled their summer days with picnics and swims in the local lake. When day ended, the family retired for the night with the front door unlocked. Since air conditioning hadn't yet made its now-essential presence felt, my grandmother hosed off the roof on hot summer days so that the house would cool by evening. A backyard filled with crabapple trees provided abundant shade—and ample opportunity for a good round of apple slinging.

Though it was a simple time, it was also a hard time.

The Great Depression had just begun, and my grandparents were forced to make a number of adjustments in order to cope with life's new scarcities. That included renting their house to a wealthy doctor and moving to simpler quarters to make ends meet. My grandmother, a woman my mother described as an astute businessperson, stretched the few dollars Grandpa brought home each week.

December 1932 brought Seattle's usual dose of rain and bluster. My mother was fourteen years old that year, and next to youngest in a family where it was sometimes hard to get recognition or a fair share. As Christmas approached, it became clear that the clan's few dollars wouldn't provide much in the way of new clothes or gifts. Mama already wore hand-me-downs. New clothes would have been a Christmas blessing, but this year, the holidays wouldn't mean goodies under the tree. And yet, as always, there would be riches in the form of good but simple fare, dear friends, and family love.

It grieved my mother that her one gift under the Christmas tree that year was a single pair of underpants. Though disappointed, she derived some sense of pleasure in the fact that they were hers and hers alone. No one else had ever worn them.

"They were brand new," she said proudly, as she recapped the holiday for me many years later. "And," she added, the corners of her mouth turning up into a soft smile, "they were all mine."

Mama understood the underpants were practical—as were each of the gifts her siblings received. She knew also that necessities came first when money was scarce. But understanding and accepting isn't always enough. She recalls shedding a secret tear over her gift, the one piece of clothing that hadn't even entered her mind when she thought of all the possibilities that might await her beneath the Christmas tree.

After she contained her disappointment and set it aside, she opened her heart to the holiday and allowed something else to touch her deeply that day. Laughter enveloped her as family and friends gathered to share the warmth, the chilly rain outside notwithstanding. She remembers how her sister, Isabelle, had banged out the carols on the piano, an instrument the family had managed to retain, and how everyone gave Christmas renditions their all. She recalls how pleased everyone had been that Grandma had once again shown an uncanny ability to produce something from nothing, gracing the table with a small turkey. As she retells the story, she says she could almost hear the chatter and laughter that blotted out the paucity of culinary luxuries as the family sat down to eat that day so long ago.

Far from being bereft that day, she had in fact been the recipient of a great gift. She learned the true meaning of Christmas, and that's something she will never forget or take for granted.

Holiday Visitors

BY MICHAEL M. ALVAREZ

I pull up slowly and stop near the chained gate. For the hundredth time, I read the sign: KEEP OUT PRIVATE PROPERTY. As I wait for my friends, Larry and Tony, to arrive, I glance at the house again.

Old Man Valentine's house hasn't changed much since I was a child. It still looks a little scary. I smile as I recall the first time we ventured onto that porch. It had been 1964, and we were fearless.

"I dare you!" Tony said.

"I double dare you," Larry added.

I stood between the two best friends any eleven year old could have, and swallowed the huge lump in my dry throat. It was two days before Christmas, and everyone was getting ready for the holidays. Mom was baking, and I had just helped Dad put up the foil tree with the rotating colored lights. We three boys had found a few minutes to ourselves, and had walked directly to this house as if pulled there by some invisible force.

"C'mon, Mikey, you gonna stand there all day or you gonna go up and knock on the door?" Tony challenged.

"I'll go if you guys come with me," I answered.

"Okay," they agreed.

Slowly, one cautious step at a time, we moved toward the house that most people in town swore was haunted. The story was that when Old Man Valentine's wife was alive, they were both happy and friendly with everyone in town. Then Mrs. Valentine got sick. No one really knew what was wrong with her, but after a while, neither of them left the house. Some days, Old Man Valentine went into town to buy groceries and pay bills, but the rest of the time he and his wife stayed inside their big, rambling house.

A few years later, someone in town said they'd heard from Doc Johnson that Mrs. Valentine had died. Someone else said Old Man Valentine went crazy and kept his wife's body somewhere inside the scary old house. Perhaps, they said, he might have buried her in the backyard.

When we finally stood in front of the splintered front door, we blinked rapidly, hoping we weren't making a mistake. Taking a deep breath, I gave Tony and Larry a thumbs-up sign, and we all knocked on the door at the same time.

"Go away!" bellowed Old Man Valentine from behind the door.

Though ready to run, we stood our ground. In the next heartbeat, the front door screeched and began to open slowly. We could see only darkness beyond. We waited a moment, wondering if we had really heard a voice or if we had imagined it. From somewhere in the darkness, the voice sounded again, friendlier this time.

"Well, might as well come in, boys. And close that door—it's freezing outside."

We looked at one another, our eyes huge in our pale faces. Once we had stepped inside, the front door swung shut. *Trapped!* my mind screamed. The only moment of clarity I recall was a question that repeated over and over in my mind: *What would the Lone Ranger do?*

I didn't have time to figure it out, because the voice came again.

"I'm in the kitchen, boys. Just follow the light," the voice said. I looked at Tony and Larry. I'm sure the Lone Ranger would have gotten more details before he followed that shaft of light, but when my friends started moving toward the voice, I went with them. The aroma of freshly baked cookies reached us as we neared the light.

When we peeked inside the kitchen, we were startled to see an elderly man with white hair opening the oven door. Old Man Valentine didn't look like a monster. He was old, but he didn't look like any of us had imagined. He was a little hunched over, and used a walking cane that was carved out of mesquite. He looked up and nodded.

"Just in time, my friends," he said, as he pulled a tray of cookies from an ancient oven. "I'd like your opinion on my pumpkin cookies. I tried to follow Millie's recipe, but I'm afraid I'm not as good a cook as she was." He moved to the table and sat down.

We stood in the doorway, tongue-tied. Finally, we moved to the table and joined him.

Tony's tongue came untied first. "You don't look crazy."

The way Old Man Valentine stared at Tony, I thought we were goners for sure, but the strangest thing happened. The old man threw back his head and belted out the biggest laugh I'd ever heard!

When he was able to stop laughing, he smiled. "I'm not crazy, boys. Guess just a bit lonely most of the time. When I think of Millie being gone, I get a bit sad, but I ain't crazy."

"This is good!" Larry said, munching a cookie.

The cookies were good. Tony and I slowly chewed one cookie, swallowed it carefully, and then tried another.

"Sorry," the old man said, shrugging his shoulders. "I don't have any milk."

We were perfectly happy without milk, but before we could say so, Tony blurted out another question, which had us squirming in our chairs.

"So where's your wife?" Tony asked, as he took another bite of his cookie.

The old man leaned on his cane and gently shook his head. "Suppose in the same cemetery where she was buried twenty years ago. Got cancer, Millie did. 'Course the docs didn't know what to do in those days. All they could do was watch her fade away." Mr. Valentine looked at the floor, his lips drawn tight.

I swallowed the cookie and then cleared my throat. "I'm sorry about your wife."

A sad smile appeared on his face and he looked up at me. "I miss her the most around the holidays. Millie loved cooking during the holidays," he murmured, then went silent again.

That day, in 1964, we discovered the truth about Old Man Valentine. He wasn't a mean, crazy, old man who lived in a large, spooky house. He was just a gentle, quiet man, who loved his wife very much and cherished her memory. He wasn't a man to be frightened of—he was a man who needed friends, especially around the holidays.

We made a pact that day: The three of us would always get together for the holidays and visit Mr. Valentine.

The flash of headlights interrupts my thoughts as two cars pull up. I smile when I see Tony and Larry step from their cars, ready and eager—as am I—for another holiday visit with Mr. Valentine.

Home for the Holidays

BY WAYNE R. WALLACE

I was nineteen years old when I shipped out to basic training at Lackland Air Force Base in San Antonio, Texas. Away
from home for the first time, those six weeks of training passed
quickly. From there, I received orders to go to Gunter AFB in
Alabama, for training as a medical corpsman.

When we arrived, our technical school was closed for the
Christmas holiday. We were placed on PAT—Personnel Awaiting Training—status until after New Year's Day. This meant
spending every other day on twelve hours of K.P.—washing
dishes, cleaning up the mess hall, and anything else the mess
sergeants didn't want to do themselves. The days in between,
however, were spent helping out with various assignments
that ranged from picking up trash to actual office duties. It
made for a nice change of pace, but now that the newness of
being in the service had begun to wear off, I thought more and
more about home. What I wouldn't give to have the chance to
visit home before I was sent overseas . . . and Christmas was
coming up.

One afternoon, I drew the lucky card. I got the job of filling in as "gopher" for one of the colonels on the base. I was
to answer the phone and take messages on a yellow tablet

for him while he spent the day on leisurely time off, playing golf.

I settled into the big leather chair behind the Colonel's desk that morning and began my duties. I answered calls, writing out the Colonel's messages in my very best script, in the hopes that I might get asked back for this cushy job. Around mid-morning, an Air Force Reserve Major at Tinker AFB in Oklahoma City called.

"Tell the Colonel that we have sixty-five Air Force Reservists training there at Gunter from the Oklahoma City area," he said. "They've been away from home for a few months, and if he will be kind enough to grant them leave, we'll send a transport jet to pick them up on December 20th. Since their school is closed for the holidays, this will allow them to spend Christmas with their families, and we'll bring them back right before New Year's." He waited a moment, then asked, "Have you got all that?"

I must have hesitated for a moment before answering, because I couldn't believe my ears! Oklahoma City was my hometown, too! "Y-Yes, sir, I have it all," I stammered. "I'll relate this to the Colonel as soon as he returns. Thank you very much, sir!"

This was just too good to be true. Granted, there were a few problems involved. First, the Major had mentioned *just* Air Force Reservists who were on the base. I was *regular* Air Force. At that time, the Vietnam War made getting into the reserves an extremely hard task. Reservist positions were filled by the sons of politicians and other privileged persons who did not care to visit the jungles of Vietnam. I had not been one of the fortunate. Being regular Air Force, I was a prime candidate for Asian duty. This would probably be my last Christmas stateside for a very long time. And I wanted to go home.

"The uniform's the same," I said aloud to convince myself it could be done. "Who'll ever know?"

As soon as the Colonel returned, I jumped to attention and saluted him smartly. I took his coat and hung it up, then began to relate his messages. When I got to the message from Tinker AFB, his reaction stunned me.

"Damn," he said, shaking his head in disbelief. "They sure spoil those weekend warriors! I have a good notion to deny them leave and make them stay here!"

My heart sank.

The Colonel read the disappointment on my face and said, "What's the problem, airman?"

"Sir, Oklahoma City is my hometown, too. My mother is there, and my sweetheart. I would kill to get on that airplane," I answered honestly.

"But you're *regular* Air Force, son," the Colonel reminded me. "That plane's for those reservist pansies!"

"I know, sir, and you know . . . but they'd never know!"

He grinned, and began handwriting a memo. "Give this to the Sergeant at the orderly room and have him notify the reservist's commander of this opportunity. While you're at it, have him type you a leave slip so you can go, too."

"Oh, thank you, sir!" I said.

"It does my heart good to be able to send a regular on that Christmas flight with that bunch of weekenders!" the Colonel said.

I ran out the door to the orderly room a block away. When I got there, a cigar-chomping Master Sergeant sat behind the desk, and seemed to be in a terrible mood. I handed him the handwritten memo.

"No-good weekend warriors!" he grunted. "Nobody seems interested in sending *my* troops home to see their mommies," he snapped sarcastically, and began to pound out the memo on an ancient Royal typewriter. I stood, waiting for him to finish.

"What are you waiting for, airman?" the Sergeant growled around his cigar.

"Well, Sergeant," I said nervously, "the Colonel told me to have you type a leave authorization for me so I could go, too."

The Sergeant threw his head back and laughed. "Yeah, sure he did. I'll believe that when *he* tells me. Now get out of here."

I was devastated. I went back to the Colonel's office and reported that the memo had been delivered.

"Well, shouldn't you be at the barracks packing?" he asked.

"Sir, the Sergeant didn't believe me. He said he'd believe it when he heard it from *you*."

Without a word, the Colonel reached for the phone and dialed the orderly room.

"Sergeant," he snapped, "I'm sending Airman Wallace back over there and you *will* drop everything else you might be doing and immediately type this young man's leave authorization. *Is that understood?*" He hung up without waiting for an answer. Then he looked at me. "Now, go get that leave paper and have a Merry Christmas."

I rushed back to the orderly room and found the Master Sergeant sitting in a cloud of cigar smoke, typing my leave authorization. He glanced up at me and frowned. "Airman Wallace," he said slowly, as if to memorize my name, "I will remember this incident. Screw up just one time while you're here, and I'll have you out on Air Force garbage collection duty so fast you won't believe it!"

I nodded and accepted the leave with wings on my feet. He could have threatened to shoot me—I wouldn't have cared. I was going home for Christmas!

Some Gifts Cannot Be Wrapped

BY LYNNE COOPER SITTON

Grandmother dozed in her armchair, her head dropping onto her chest. She resembled a papoose wrapped in layers of cloth. Her shawl covered her boney shoulders, and a thick afghan spread across her lap and wound around her legs. Despite dry heat spewing from the radiator beside her, Grandmother looked like she belonged in an igloo. The unmistakable odor of antiseptic and urine clung to everything in the tiny nursing home room she shared with a bedridden roommate.

My two young sons knew the rules for obligatory visits with their ninety-five-year-old great-grandmother: no bickering, speak clearly, and don't ask when we're leaving.

As the boys waited for my signal to enter, Grandmother stirred, opened her eyes, and smiled a toothless grin I hardly recognized as hers.

"Lynne, dear!" She motioned us closer with an emaciated hand. "And Jay and Andrew! What a nice surprise."

"We've come with some Christmas cheer," I said, placing a windowsill-sized arrangement of holly and pine beside her as I kissed her withered cheek.

Glancing around the room, I noticed three Christmas cards on her small bookcase and felt a shroud of sadness descend. She had outlived almost everyone who had sent greetings in past years. Grandmother's two favorite pictures hung on the wall and several family photos fought for space among the tissue box, magnifying glass, napkins, and plastic cups on her nightstand. These few personal touches, and Grandmother's overstuffed armchair, failed to overcome the drab institutional beige.

The boys sat dutifully on Grandmother's tightly made hospital bed, and I, glancing at my watch to note "appropriate visiting time," grabbed the only remaining chair in the room. Grandmother nodded appreciatively while I gave her a rundown about family activities, the boys' school projects, and Christmas dinner at my parents' house.

"We're looking forward to having you with us," I said, preparing to leave. "Nobody in the family can make gravy like you do!" Rumor had it that my grandmother had never made a batch of lumpy gravy in her life.

As I stood to go, Grandmother motioned me to her side and hissed in my ear, "Lynne, dear, do you have two dollars I can borrow?"

I frowned. *Why would she need money?* "I've got a five or ten dollar bill," I whispered back, just loud enough for the hearing aid. "Will that do?"

"No," she sighed. "Just two dollar bills."

"Are you sure?" I asked.

"Yes, dear." Grandmother seemed very disappointed.

As she answered, her eyes swept over my sons. I looked from her to them and back again, and her odd request suddenly burst into a heart-wrenching realization: She wanted one dollar for each of her great-grandsons; she had nothing to give them!

"Just a second," I said to Grandmother and my sons, "I'll be right back."

I strode down the cheerless hall into a Christmas fairyland of poinsettias, multicolored lights, and wreaths that decorated the nurse's station. Hundreds of images of Grandmother's presence in my life tumbled through my mind. My sons would never know their great-grandmother as I did. They saw only a wizened old lady, caught without gifts to give, in the shadows of her last years. They hadn't jumped rope with her when she turned sixty. They had never seen the exquisitely embroidered bodice of my wedding gown or the colorful pillowcases with my name on them that were my childhood treasures. The boys didn't know her favorite flowers were violets, or that she had survived diphtheria, and had been tossed out of a run-away horse and buggy as a child. They had never seen Grandmother cut sandwiches into smiley faces so they tasted better. They didn't know she had hand-stitched hundreds of tiny doll clothes for her granddaughters, *and* matching Christmas outfits for us. They didn't know who taught me to embroider or told me all the funny family stories. They had never tasted her amazing made-from-scratch desserts or seen one of Grandmother's beautiful crepe-paper flower arrangements. My boys saw only the wrinkled exterior wrapping of one of my life's richest blessings.

"Change for a five?" I asked as I held the bill toward a heavyset nurse at the console. Her red-and-green bell earrings tinkled as she retrieved a few crumpled dollar bills from a zippered bag.

"Here you are, honey," she said with a grin.

I smiled my thanks and hurried back to Grandmother's room, secretly slipping four of the five bills into her hand. Grandmother gave me a grateful nod, and then offered her gifts to Jay and Andrew. The boys were gracious, but I knew they weren't exactly overwhelmed by two dollars.

Right then and there, I decided my sons needed to discover who their great-grandmother really was. Grandmother's faith, wisdom, heritage, knowledge, and experiences sparkled far more beautifully than anything we could wrap and place beneath a Christmas tree.

Despite the boys' obvious glares, I pulled my chair closer to Grandmother's chair and asked her to tell us how she had been kicked in the stomach by a cow when she was Andrew's age. That story unlocked a treasure chest of other stories, lessons, people, and experiences that had occurred throughout her life. Andrew and Jay hung on her every word, asking questions and laughing along with her. I moderated—prompting her to tell one story after another.

The sparkle in Grandmother's eyes as she shared her memories that afternoon bridged another generation. A lump grew in my throat at the expression of rapt attention I saw on my sons' faces. They would remember much more than a stuffy nursing home when they thought of their great-grandmother in years to come, and by the look on Grandmother's face, I knew the gift they had given her that Christmas was priceless.

In the Nick of Time

by Mimi Greenwood Knight

I was ten the year God sent grandchildren to Mama for Christmas. My little sister Betsy was seven. We were the babies in a family of twelve and, since we were both newly hip to the whole Santa thing, it would be the first Christmas in twenty years that Mama wasn't playing Santa to someone. At the time, my brother, Wayne, was the only sibling with children, and he and his wife had recently transferred clear across the country to California. Though Mama tried not to let it show, we knew she was depressed.

On Christmas Eve, my siblings and I sat around the living room talking about our nieces, wondering what they were doing. We imagined how empty the next day would be without them. When we couldn't stand it any longer, we telephoned and passed the phone around the room, each in turn asking the girls if they'd been good and what they hoped Santa would leave under their tree. Mama pretended not to hear as she busied herself in the kitchen.

We had no way of knowing that a miracle lay in store for us, or that within the next few hours we would discover first-hand that God indeed works in mysterious ways.

We lived on a busy state highway in a section of the road known to local residents as Dead Man's Curve. The title was no joke. A man once died in Dad's arms right on our front lawn after being hit by a car as he walked along that treacherous strip of highway. The sound of screeching tires and smashing steel was not unusual to our family. Over the years, many strangers had found refuge on our living room couch waiting for an ambulance, tow truck, or family member to rescue them.

That Christmas Eve, just as we hung up the phone, the familiar sound of screeching tires reached us. We held our breath, waiting for the second sound—the ear-slitting crash that indicated an accident had taken place. Collectively, we bolted for the front door. How anyone walked away from this one was the first part of our miracle. An eighteen-wheeler had slammed into a station wagon holding a young couple and their two tiny daughters. By the time we got there, the truck was on its side in the ditch. The station wagon had crossed the road, plowed through the ditch, and landed scant inches from a row of trees. We stared in awe as the truck driver and the young family crawled from the wreckage. Despite the extensive damage to the vehicles, none of the passengers had been injured.

As another driver controlled the traffic, Mama and Dad hustled everyone into the house. While Dad called the police, Mama warmed up dinner. The truck driver got picked up right away, but the family was stranded. They had been on their way to Mississippi to spend the holiday with elderly grandparents, who had no means of rescuing them.

It took our family all of three seconds to fall in love with those two little girls who were about the same ages as my nieces. Mama scrounged around in her closet and found some toys. Then she wrapped and stashed them under the tree as

Santa gifts for our visitors. She even found a little something for their mom and dad.

My sister and I, pleased to have the company, gave them our bed and slept on the den floor. Mama rocked the baby to sleep, while Dad read Christmas stories to her sister. Long after my siblings and I had drifted off to sleep, Mama's sewing machine whirred.

When we woke the next morning, Dad read the Christmas Story from the bible and the three-year-old placed the figures in the manger the way we used to when we were little. The Christmas tree was surrounded by presents that hadn't been there before. With wide eyes, we smiled at Mama in amazement. She had made a painting smock and a small dress and pinafore for the little girl, as well as a Christmas apron for the child's mother and a bonnet for her baby sister! Though she must have stayed up all night sewing, she was all smiles as the family accepted their gifts.

Around noon the next day, someone arrived from Mississippi to pick up our guests. But by then the miracle had already taken place—the strangers in our home were no longer strangers. After that, the little family was a regular presence on Christmas Eve. Even after their grandparents had passed on and the family no longer had reason to travel in our direction, they stayed in touch through Christmas cards and occasional visits.

Now, as I spend Christmases with my own four children, I reflect often on the Christmas miracle of 1970. God prevented anyone from being injured that day, and in the process He healed Mama's heart by sending her what she needed most at that moment in time—grandchildren.

The Hairbrush

BY BOB ROSE

Because it would be the family's first Christmas without my mother, none of us knew what to expect that December. Since my earliest memories, Mom had been the hostess for all of our holiday gatherings. But seeing how lost we all were this year, my wife, Kathy, stepped up to the plate and took over.

She prepared Thanksgiving dinner at our house that year, which helped make the transition for the first holiday without Mom. But, despite Kathy's efforts, in our hearts none of us were sure what to expect when we once again congregated at Dad's house for Christmas.

Dad did his best to make the place festive. He dug out all the Christmas decorations and placed them where he remembered them being in previous years. He even gathered evergreen boughs to line the mantel, and then placed the ceramic "Santa Claus Sleeping in a Chair," painted by Mom before I was born, among the needles. The Nativity set that had graced their home since the Christmas of 1945 held a place of honor on the sideboard in the dining room. When Kathy and I and our three boys arrived from our home, some eight hours distant, we took on the task of decorating the seven-foot-tall Douglas fir Dad had purchased. Memories flooded my mind as we placed the ornaments on the tree. Each one held a story and invoked a different and unique memory that included Mom.

On Christmas Eve, Kathy again stepped in and prepared a scrumptious turkey dinner with all the trimmings. Careful to keep tradition strong, she served dinner on the dining room table that had once been my grandparents'—even Mom's favorite salt and pepper shakers, purchased in the late 1940s, a snowman and a Christmas tree, were on the table, as always. Dad set a fire in the fireplace, and Christmas music played softly in the background, compliments of the collection of *Goodyear* Christmas records my folks had amassed over the years.

Immediately after dinner, we bundled up the children and headed for Christmas Eve services at the community church that had been our family's place of worship for three generations. We exited the white steeple-topped church with the sounds of the glorious traditional carols of the day echoing in our hearts, and arrived home to the lingering smells of turkey and dressing, the fire in the fireplace, and the freshly cut evergreen tree. By this time, our boys—ages seven, three, and ten months—were anxious to get into the living room to open their presents.

Everything was as it should be—with the exception that Mom wasn't there.

The boys' excitement overcame the pall created by Mom's absence, and we all found ourselves caught up in their delight. Our eldest son, Justin, a first grader and beginning reader, played Santa. Soon all the gifts had been delivered.

When most of the gifts had been opened, I spied something behind the tree.

"Santa," I said, as Justin tore into his first package, "I think you missed one."

Justin conducted a final check, spotted the present, and crawled to the back of the tree to retrieve it. The tag read, To JUSTIN—FROM GRANDMA.

We all stared at the box as Justin ripped away the paper, until all that was left in his hand was a red-and-blue Superman hairbrush—the perfect present for a little boy just assuming his own grooming duties. Tears formed in Dad's eyes.

"Mom evidently purchased the brush the previous spring," he explained. "Then wrapped it, and stowed it in the hall closet to be retrieved at Christmastime. I found it a few weeks ago and waited until no one was looking to slip it under the tree for Justin to discover."

Because my parents lived in rural Wyoming, a hundred miles from the closest mall, Mom had always made the most of every shopping trip. She often bought gifts well in advance and stashed them away. The hairbrush for her eldest grandson was her last such purchase.

I put my arm around Justin as he ran the brush through his hair for the first time, and I saw the smile appear on his face—tentative at first, then growing into an ear-to-ear grin. It was the same grin I'd seen on his face before, when his grandmother had placed her hand on his head gently and combed her fingers through his blonde hair. And it brought about a moment of understanding for all of us: It made us realize you can never really lose someone you love.

Without a doubt, the first Christmas we spent without Mom was a tough one. But when Justin opened the box containing the Superman hairbrush, a rush of reality enveloped us. *Mom's love would always be with us.* And now, thirty years later, I can honestly say not a Christmas has gone by since when we haven't thought of that hairbrush and what it meant to each of us on that very tough first Christmas.

Mother Nature to the Rescue

BY GEORGIA A. HUBLEY

I remember Saturday morning, December 15, 1945 as if it were yesterday. I jumped out of bed, giddy with happiness. While it was not Christmas Day, it was an exciting day. It was the day for my family's Christmas tradition—going to the woods and cutting down an old-fashioned Christmas tree!

"Don't forget to wear your heavy mittens," Mom said. "You don't want your hands to get cold or have your fingers pricked by the cedar-tree branches."

As I put on my mittens, I thought of all the paper-bird decorations I'd be making for the tree. Mom had already strung popcorn into garlands, but we would also be baking gingerbread cookies, as a final touch. As always, Mom would insist *all* the cookies be hung on the tree, but we knew she'd give in and let us sample one or two. Just thinking about the adventures that awaited me today brought a smile to my face. But as I raced to the stairway, I overheard a conversation that slowed my step.

"Money's scarce. There's not much money for Christmas this year," Dad said.

"Oh, don't fret," Mom replied. "We'll make do with what we have on hand. Besides, you always find a way to get us through hard times. Wait and see."

Even at the age of six, I knew what not having enough money for Christmas meant. But at that moment, chopping down our Christmas tree was all that mattered to me.

As I hurried downstairs, Dad shouted, "Let's head for the woods!" Giggling with excitement, I got in line behind Dad.

We had a system. Dad led the way with an axe in one hand and a ball of twine in the other hand. Mom, my brother, and I followed, trudging through the snow in search of the best cedar in the forest. When we reached the woods, we spotted a grove of six cedar trees.

"Pick the one you want and I'll chop it down," Dad said, standing back so we could all get a good look.

I saw an abandoned bird nest in one of the cedar trees. "Oh! Let's get this one!" I squealed. My four-year-old brother agreed.

This tree was perfect for us. It was approximately five feet tall, was irregular in shape, and had graceful dense branches adorned with clusters of prickly, bur-like, dark-green foliage. I was glad Mom reminded me to wear my heavy mittens!

After Dad chopped down the cedar tree, he wrapped twine around it several times and then tied the end of the twine into a long handle so we could all help carry our load. I peeked at the bird nest tucked in the branches and shivered with excitement as I visualized my very own folded, white paper dove sitting in it.

As we neared our farmhouse, we heard a car horn honk repeatedly. Looking around, we spotted a man and woman, whom we didn't recognize, standing beside a car parked on the gravel road that ran parallel with our farm.

Dad squinted at them through the bright sunlight. Then he lowered the tree to the ground. "They must be stuck in a snowdrift," he said.

We quickly leaned the cedar against a snow-covered tree stump and turned to offer our help. Bur rather than wait for us to come to them, the couple climbed over the split rail fence and walked toward us.

When they were close enough to be heard clearly, the man looked at Dad. "Did you chop down your own Christmas tree?"

"We sure did," Dad said. "Are you having car trouble?"

The man smiled. "No. We've come to the country to find a special Christmas tree. We were hoping you could help us." He looked from Dad to Mom, hopefully. "We'll pay you." Stretching his hand out to shake my father's hand, he introduced himself. "Name's Jim, and this here's Emma."

After introductions were made Dad smiled, looked at our tree, and then back at the couple. "How 'bout a cedar?"

"No," Jim said with a confident shake of his head. "We'd like a dead tree."

We looked at him in surprise.

"You really want a dead tree for a Christmas tree?" Dad asked.

"Yes," Emma said, "with smooth branches that can be displayed on a table."

Mom's brow puckered. "How do you decorate a dead tree?"

"We wrap each branch in cotton to resemble snow, and then decorate it with real bird nests that we've collected in our travels." She glanced at the surrounding countryside and inhaled deeply as if she enjoyed the out-of-doors. "And we attach dried leaves, flowers, and bird ornaments on the branches. It's to be a Mother Nature's Christmas tree."

Never having heard of such a tree, my parents and brothers had gone quite silent. But when I thought about it, I decided it probably would be a wonderful tree. *Hadn't we just chosen our tree because it had a bird nest in it?*

"We have a bird nest in our tree, too." I offered.

Emma's eyes lit up. She looked at me eagerly. "Would you like to sell it?"

Immediately, I regretted mentioning the bird nest. At the same time, I remembered the conversation I'd just heard in the house—money was scarce. *Would I lose our bird nest?* Instead of answering her, I blinked to keep the tears from falling.

"Our bird nest isn't for sale," Dad said. Pointing his axe toward the woods, he signaled everyone to follow. "Come, let's go to the woods and see if Mother Nature has a tree waiting for you."

I smiled. My dad knew the bird nest is what made *our* tree special, too!

As soon as we found a dead tree, we hauled it back to their car where Dad helped them stuff it carefully into the trunk so the branches wouldn't break.

Then Jim turned to Dad, "Thank you for helping us find our tree. Here's $20 for your trouble. Merry Christmas!"

I smiled as Dad and Jim shook hands again. I knew $20 was a lot of money—surely it was enough so that money wouldn't be scarce at our house for Christmas.

Dad smiled at Mom as he stuffed the money in his pocket.

Mom smiled back. "You always find a way to get us through hard times."

Dad grinned and gave Mom a hug. Then he looked back at the woods and shouted at the top of his lungs, "Thank you, Mother Nature. Merry Christmas!"

Dancing with Daddy

by Marilyn Olsein

Living in a small town in Texas during World War II was tough, especially at Christmas. My father, disqualified from the Armed Forces because of his age, was working in an auto factory in Michigan, trying to earn more money than farming paid.

When I remember my childhood, the phrase "dirt poor" comes to mind, but we—Mama, my brother, my two sisters, and me—always managed a wonderful Christmas. Mama's family came to our house for dinner, and Mama made pans of Swedish cardamom rolls, the sweet smell filling the whole house. Grampa would bring in a couple of chickens for Mama to roast and fry, and we'd have cornbread dressing, white and sweet potatoes, corn, and green beans that Gramma had canned. We ate, laughed, sang, and carried on all day and into the night.

Not long after that hateful war ended, Mama sat us down on the screened porch and told us we'd spend our next Christmas in Michigan. We were moving to Detroit to be with Daddy.

I was terrified. We all were—even Mama, I think. Detroit was at least a hundred thousand times bigger than Melvin, Texas.

"Mama, doesn't it snow up there . . . a lot?" Phyllis asked. At twelve, she was the eldest.

I was born in Texas and, at the age of seven, I could remember seeing snow only once—the Christmas the Army gave all my uncles holiday leave. Uncle Steve, Mama's youngest brother and my favorite, chased me down a slippery road and washed my face with a handful of cold, melting flakes.

"It's not like snow in Texas," I said. "Detroit snow is black."

"Don't tell fibs, Marilyn," Mama scolded. "Snow is white, wherever it falls."

"Maybe it's white when it first comes down in Detroit, but Daddy's letter said coal smoke from the factories makes it black," I insisted. I imagined Detroit as a city without color, all black, gray, and white.

"You'll find out soon enough," Mama said. "We'll be in Detroit for the first snowfall." She saw my face cloud up. "And crying won't change things."

I didn't want to spend Christmas in a cold, dirty city with a stranger, for that's what Daddy had become to me.

Daddy immigrated to the States from Sweden as a grown man. When I was three, he left Texas, tenant farming, and us to work "Up North." He planned to earn enough money to send for us. First, he worked in the shipyards in Portland, Oregon, then in an auto factory in Detroit. During the four years we were separated, I forgot what he looked like. What turned out to be worse, I forgot what he sounded like.

When we got off the train in Detroit, Mama hugged and kissed Daddy and then introduced us girls. He didn't need to be reminded of his son's name—his namesake. He spoke to me first, and held out his arms. I started to cry and held tight to Mama's hand.

My young ears had learned to understand a Texas drawl with a slight Swedish accent—my mother and her family are also Swedish. Daddy's thicker accent had taken on a completely foreign Yankee twang. I didn't understand him. None of us did, except Mama, and his frustration was intense.

For weeks, Mama spoke to him in Swedish and then told us in English what he'd said. It was almost Christmas before I could understand him quickly enough to keep him from yelling for Mama whenever he tried to say anything to me.

A few days after Thanksgiving, Daddy was included in a layoff. We were eating breakfast, getting ready for school, when Mama sat down next to me—something she'd never done. My heart fell into my stomach, and I couldn't take another bite of cocoa and toast. I had a feeling something awful was coming.

"There won't be much Christmas this year," she said slowly.

"I'm being good, Mama," Eric said.

"Yes, you are, but Daddy lost his job for a little while. It's so the auto company won't have to give him holiday pay. They'll hire him back after New Year's, but right now, it'll take all our money to buy groceries, pay the rent, and keep coal in the furnace."

"That's okay," I said through my tears. "We'll have a big one next year."

I didn't know it at the time, but back then, Detroit had an old newsboy organization called *The Goodfellows*. Daddy swallowed his pride and put our names on their "Needy Kids" list.

Goodfellows gave Eric a toy car. Phyllis, Sonja, and I got dolls, each one different. It was the only doll I ever got for Christmas. Because the gift hadn't come from my parents, I almost felt disloyal when I held her in my arms. I still remember her silky blonde hair and ruffled blue dress, and how perfect she looked.

On Christmas morning, I woke to the sound of music I remembered hearing when I was little. Daddy was in the kitchen, listening to a radio station that played Swedish music! I slipped out of bed and peeked around the door. He began to sing in Swedish while he stirred a pot of oatmeal, then he twirled and danced a schottische around the kitchen. I was overflowing with happiness at the familiar sounds and sights. Watching Daddy dancing alone made me giggle out loud.

"God Jul, litet dotter," he said and swept me up in his thick arms.

"Merry Christmas, Daddy!" I responded happily.

I held tight to his neck, and laughed while he sang, as we spun around the kitchen floor. I smelled his spicy aftershave and rested my cheek against the coarseness of a beard he could never completely shave off.

It no longer mattered that the snow wasn't white, that the day was cold and gray, or even that the beautiful doll was a gift from strangers. It was Christmas morning, and I was dancing with the Daddy I remembered.

The Sweeping Angel

by Rita H. Strong

Every first grader in the parochial school I attended back in the '30s, was in the Christmas pageant. I was chosen to be one of the many angels—a kitchen one at that. There were shepherds, Wise Men, and Mary and Joseph, as well as herald angels. A baby doll was going to be Jesus.

My mother trimmed my flowing pink angel gown with gold rickrack around the bottom and at the elbow-length sleeves. The other angels wore white gowns, also trimmed in gold. Our teacher had shredded white crepe paper for feathers and glued it on cardboard wings. Halos were embroidery hoops, wrapped with gold tinsel rope. The little broom I was to use had the same glittering rope wrapped around the handle. Everyone had a part in the play. I got to be the Sweeping Angel.

The night before the pageant, Mother put my poker-straight brown hair in rags. I had fat sausage curls the next morning and felt and looked my best!

I still recall exactly how it all was to take place . . .

When the curtain rose, I would be sweeping bits of hay on the floor near the Holy Family, just as they are seen on Christmas cards. The shepherds, led by the other angels, would sing, "Where are we going? Where are we going?" to the tune of "Frere Jacques." The angels accompanying them would answer, "To the stable, to the stable. You're going to see Jesus! You're going to see Jesus!" Then everybody would join in and we'd all sing, "He is born! He is born!"

At that point, a shepherd would rap at the imitation stable door. As I hurried across the stage with my broom, I would call twice, "Who is there?" and then wait for the answer. When I heard the shepherd call out, "Shepherds," I would open the door and say, "Come in!"

At that point, Mary would pick up the Baby Jesus doll and ask, "Have you come to see our baby?" Joseph would say, "His name is Jesus." All together, we would sing, "Shepherds, what did you see?" Then the Wise Men would come with their gifts. One would say, "I bring gold," the second one would say, "I bring frankincense," and the third would say, "I bring myrrh." As Mary lay the baby down, she would say, "We have had so much company, Jesus is sleepy." Then we'd all sing a Christmas lullaby and another carol.

After that, the play would be over.

But . . . the stable door stuck when I tried to open it. The shepherd, knowing it was his cue to step into the stable, pulled on it from the opposite side. Feeling me tug on the door, he let go. The door opened with a WHOOSH! It tottered this way and that, and finally toppled with a CRASH. I jumped out of the way in time and fell down, landing on my broom. My halo flew off and dropped into my lap. Afraid I had ruined the play, my bottom lip quivered, tears imminent. But when I realized that everyone was laughing, I laughed too.

Our teacher, watching our antics from backstage, quickly remedied the problem by sending one of the eighth-grade boys onto the stage to remove the offending door. While the door was being taken care of, I stood up and brushed myself off. As soon as I could, I located my halo and plopped it back on my head. Then, with a giggle, I picked up my broom and said to the shepherd, whom I could clearly see waiting for his cue to enter, "Come in."

Thankfully, the play continued with no more surprises.

When the play was over and the curtain had come down, the audience clapped and clapped. Even though this play had been seen many times before, the audience was heard to say they felt this time they had seen the best performers—especially the little Sweeping Angel who fell.

An Inexpensive Gift

BY MATTHIAS L. NISKA

Christmas is a big deal at Concordia College, my alma mater. Each December, the quaint little campus, nestled in the heart of residential Moorhead, amid the prairies of northwestern Minnesota, comes alive with holiday festivities—most of them stemming from the school's Scandinavian Lutheran heritage.

At the heart of this celebration, is the Concordia Christmas Concert, a tradition eighty years strong, in which nearly 500 student musicians—five choirs, a handbell ensemble, and a full symphony orchestra—tell the Christmas story with sacred music, old and new, enveloped by a dynamically lit, hand-painted, 150-foot-wide mural backdrop. More than 20,000 people a year flock to sold-out performances in Moorhead and at Orchestra Hall in Minneapolis, and thousands more are exposed to the concert through nationwide radio and television broadcasts. This grand tradition, which has been called Concordia's "Christmas Gift to the Midwest," is truly an impressive vehicle for community outreach. I was lucky enough to take part in this tradition for four years, and some of my most treasured memories of college come from participating in these concerts.

But not all gifts come in such large packages.

The week after the Christmas Concert during my junior year, our choir director, Dr. René Clausen, suggested that we take time out of our hectic end-of-the-semester schedules and visit a nearby nursing home to do some caroling. Even though final exams loomed just around the corner, more than half the choir took him up on his suggestion. We rehearsed for a few minutes in the choir room beforehand, learning the harmony parts to a dozen or so well-known carols, and then bundled up in our coats, hats, and gloves, and walked the few blocks to the Eventide Lutheran Home, where a perky staff member greeted us at the door.

"You're the folks from Concordia!" she said with a broad smile. "Come right in. They're waiting for you!"

She showed us to the cafeteria, a spacious open room whose off-white walls were crowded with handmade, childish decorations. A small, neatly furnished Christmas tree stood in one corner, next to a rickety upright piano. Seated all around the room, on benches and chairs and in wheelchairs, a sizable contingent of residents waited eagerly for the concert to commence.

"It's a pleasure to be here tonight, to share with you some of the best-loved carols of the season," said Dr. Clausen. "Feel free to join in if you like." With that, we began to sing.

The residents listened intently at first, their white heads bobbing in approval, their lined faces wearing expressions of cheerful nostalgia. Despite Dr. Clausen's invitation, they didn't join in at first, either because they wanted to sit back and enjoy the sonority of our well-blended voices, or out of a sense of good old-fashioned Midwestern reticence. But after three or four songs, we began to hear a few stray voices singing along, and soon nearly everyone was taking part.

It was heartwarming to see not only the joy these seniors took from the familiar music, but also how nimbly their minds recalled the melodies and lyrics they had learned as young children. Many of them probably had problems with their memories, but they knew their Christmas carols.

After about forty-five minutes, it was time for us to go. We had to get back to preparing for final exams, and the nursing home staff would be serving dinner soon. As we left, we took time to mingle with the residents, who told us how much they appreciated our music. Several said they had sung in choirs when they were younger, and a few of them were even Concordia graduates.

The choir members gradually dispersed and headed back to campus. I left the cafeteria with a few of my friends, planning to eat dinner with them before returning to my apartment to hit the books. As we sauntered down the shiny, antiseptic-scented corridor, chatting quietly amongst ourselves, a nursing assistant stepped out of one of the rooms and beckoned to us.

"Myra here was wondering if you could sing her a song," the middle-aged nursing assistant said as she led us into the room. "She heard the music coming from the cafeteria, but she told me she'd really like to see you kids sing in person."

Peering into the dim lamplight, I saw Myra lying prone on a partially reclined hospital bed, sparse wisps of silver hair framing her deeply wrinkled face, an oxygen mask strapped over her nose and mouth. She turned her head as we entered, and welcomed us with a feeble, toothless little grin. Clearly, she wasn't in any shape to attend events in the cafeteria with the other residents, but she was every bit as entitled to enjoy Christmas music as they were.

"Of course we can," my friend Joe said, glancing at the rest of us for approval. We all nodded without hesitation.

"In fact," I said, realizing that my three colleagues were a soprano, an alto, and a tenor, "we just happen to have all four parts for an SATB quartet."

"Do you think you could sing 'Silent Night'?" the nursing assistant asked, her voice still hushed. "I think Myra would really like that."

"We'd love to," Andrea said.

Joe blew a C on his pitch pipe, and we began to sing. The simple chords of the beloved old Austrian carol seemed to fill the cramped room, and Myra's worn face shone with wonder and gratitude. As we sounded the last note and then stood still for a moment of reverent, introspective silence, I noticed her eyes were glistening with tears.

"Thank you, children. That was beautiful," she rasped in a voice that was almost inaudible. "It's so moving to hear young people sing. I have a granddaughter about your age, and she sometimes comes here and sings to me."

We left Myra's room a few minutes later and made our way toward the main entrance.

"You know something, guys?" I said, turning to my classmates, "It's so easy to live out our daily routine in our safe little college bubble, never wandering too far outside our comfort zone. But it sure feels good to get out and connect with people in the community every once in a while, doesn't it?"

Andrea nodded. "Especially at this time of year."

At the door, we zipped up our parkas, slipped on our mittens, and stepped into the icy December landscape. We walked in silence for a while, each lost in our own thoughts. Then Joe said, "I'm glad we got the chance to sing for Myra. It was sort of like our little Christmas gift to her."

I smiled behind my gray woolen neck scarf. "And it didn't even cost us a dime."

Miracles

BY CARRILLEE COLLINS BURKE

"A miracle is only a prayer away," the minister said. It was Christmas Eve, 1962, and one of the lowest points in my life. I would soon be divorced, money was tight, and I was alone with Cindy, my precious thirteen-month-old daughter. If anyone needed a miracle, I certainly did.

Going to the Christmas Eve candlelight service was my way of starting a vow I'd made earlier. I took Cindy with me as promised, and let the church nursery babysit her. While the minister spoke, my mind slowly began to replace his hum of words with memories of the last few months.

After eight years of marriage, my husband had fallen in love with someone else. He asked me for a divorce. Unable to afford payments, I'd been forced to give up our house and move into a small apartment. The divorce would be final on December 28.

I sighed and sank back against the hard wooden pew and thought about all my problems. During the week, Cindy was cared for by my sister, who lived several miles away. This meant I only had her with me on the weekends. The court did not approve of this arrangement, so my employer had graciously granted me two weeks leave of absence to get my chaotic life in order.

The congregation stood and began singing the first verse of "Silent Night." I hurriedly stood, opened my song book, and mumbled the words, but my mind left the music and slipped back to three nights earlier, when the night was not silent. Wind and snow had pounded against the side of my apartment building, cooling my bedroom. For hours, I paced the floor, listening to the wind, thinking about my situation, and crying. Finally, when I could no longer tolerate my misery I gave up in despair, slumped to the floor next to my bed, and in the darkness, begged God to help me.

"I need your help, God. I know I don't talk to You much, but I will change. I promise. I will go to church every chance I can and take Cindy with me. If You could just give me a hint as to what I should do or help me in any way, God, I'll be forever grateful."

I sat on the floor for a long time, waiting for some sign from Him. I knew God wouldn't answer my prayer immediately, but I needed assurance that He'd heard me. It wasn't my custom to ask for help from anyone, much less God. But suddenly, the wind stilled and the room grew warmer. I put my head back against the bed and in a whisper added, "Please, God." Then, I crawled between the cold white sheets and slept the most restful sleep I'd had in weeks.

The children's choir woke me from my thoughts. I listened as they sang. Their little arms spread wide reminded me of the yellowed antique angel that graced my treetop each year. And once again, I realized that on Christmas Day my little angel and I would be alone.

Earlier, I had purchased a cheap little lopsided tree from the Boy Scout lot on the corner and dragged it home. A couple strings of blinking lights and a lot of silver icicles would hopefully disguise its imperfections.

The singing children ended the program by blowing out their candles. I had missed most of the sermon, but not the message. I picked Cindy up from the nursery and went home to decorate the tree. While I hung lights and glass balls on the tree, Cindy squeezed the foil icicles into tiny balls and laid them on limbs within her reach. She clapped her little hands and squealed with delight at her accomplishment. I hugged her and joined in her excitement.

It was ten o'clock when I heard a tap on the kitchen door. I placed Cindy in her playpen and walked into the kitchen. I didn't expect company, and the only neighbors I knew were the couple who shared my driveway. I opened the door a crack.

"Are you Carrie Linhart?" asked a lady with a countenance as cheery looking as her voice sounded.

"Yes," I said, hesitantly. *How did this lady know me?*

"Hello, then," she said with a giggle. "Let me introduce myself. I'm Sara O'Connor. I live right back there with my family of three teens and a husband." She pointed to a house whose backyard joined the apartment complex lawn. She pulled her red wool scarf tighter around her head for protection from the snow that was now coming down in lumps. Her black coat was already white.

"How can I help you?" I asked.

"It's really how we can help each other," she said. "May I come in and explain?"

I opened the door wider and let her enter. "Now," I said, giving her a puzzled look, "what can we do for each other?"

"I heard you were looking for a babysitter. Is that true?"

"Yes, I am, but . . ."

"Good! I'm looking for a baby to sit."

"Mrs. O'Connor, is it?" I asked.

"Call me Sara, please."

I nodded. "Okay, Sara." I smiled and then frowned. "I must tell you upfront that my child is a baby girl not yet potty trained. Is that a problem for you?"

"Oh, no, that's exactly what I want—a baby to care for. I'll treat her just like you do." When I hesitated, she said, "I have references," and handed me notes with phone numbers from other mothers she'd babysat for. "All I need is a playpen and diapers. I'll take care of the rest."

I frowned. "I'm not sure. This is so sudden. I've been searching for someone for weeks—now you appear out of nowhere. And, I can't pay much." I peered at her closely. "Who did you say told you about us?"

Sara looked around my tiny kitchen and then walked into the living room. Seeing the decorated tree, she walked toward it, talking over her shoulder. "Oh, I'm not sure. I just seem to remember hearing about you . . . maybe one of my kids."

When she spotted Cindy in the playpen, she reached to her. Cindy literally jumped into Sara's arms. I was dumb-founded. Cindy was not a child who took to strangers easily.

Sara squeezed my baby against her wet coat and in a tear-ful whisper said, "Thank you, God. She is just the little, blond-haired, blue-eyed Christmas present I asked you for." Turning to me she asked, "When can I start?"

I'd never met anyone so excited to babysit! She acted as if it was a pleasure not a job. And, somehow, I believed in her.

The next day, Cindy and I celebrated Christmas with the O'Connor family. That was the start of an ongoing friendship. Back then, they not only took care of Cindy, but me, too. I know without a doubt that the O'Connor family was my answer from God.

When I think back to that night, the minister's words ring loud and clear in my head and I have to smile. He was right—a miracle really is never more than a prayer away. As I hugged my daughter tightly, I realized something else that day. I realized the spirit of Christmas was not all parties and gifts. The real miracle lived in the soul of a small child.

Yes, Deborah, There Really Is a Santa Claus

BY LINDA BRUNO

Being called to the hospital because your parents have been in an auto accident is always a scary thing. But when you're fifteen and eleven, as my sister Deborah and I were, it is more than scary—the word "terrifying" comes to mind.

It was a gorgeous Sunday afternoon, a September day filled with blue skies and promises of fun. We had gone to visit my aunt, uncle, and cousins. We had been there just a short time, when our parents decided to go out for pizza. We cousins stayed home, goofing around and generally aggravating one another as cousins do. When the phone rang mid-afternoon, we had no reason to believe that our lives were about to change forever.

My seventeen-year-old cousin, the only one who had a driver's license, drove us to the hospital. We were told that my aunt was dead and both my parents were in critical condition. My uncle, miraculously, had survived the crash with minor cuts and abrasions.

The next few days were a blur. I don't remember how we got home that night or even if we did. I don't remember how much school we missed. I do remember feeling like I was suddenly all alone in the world, even though my sister was there with me.

We were told the hospital had notified the Red Cross, who had made arrangements for our brother to be sent home from the war in Korea, not only to see his critically injured parents, but also to take care of Deborah and me.

Mom was sent home from the hospital first. Nineteen days later Dad returned home, wearing a face mask to protect his facial bones as they healed. Because Dad's jaw had been wired shut for the time being, Mom fixed food he could sip through a straw. But Dad was becoming increasingly frustrated, not only by his physical circumstances, but also his inability to go to work and earn a living—a sure sign of manhood for a male born in the mid-'20s.As a stay-at-home mom who had never learned to drive, there was no way for Mom to obtain employment to supplement our dwindling funds. There was also no way for us kids to help out. Though we lived in the country, farming season was over, and neighbors had no need for hired hands this time of year.

As Christmas drew near, any semblance of joy or antici- pation was sadly lacking in our household. There would be no gifts. There was barely enough money to keep food on the table and the heat turned on—not a thought you want to dwell on in the midst of a bitterly cold Ohio winter.

Then one bleak December evening, as we sat playing yet another game of cards to pass the time, our dog began bark- ing furiously. Since we rarely had visitors, especially on cold, dark winter nights, we assumed she must have seen a wild animal. But as her barking intensified, we all became unusu- ally still. Crime was nearly unheard of in our neck of the woods, but you could never be too sure. *Had someone heard about our situation and decided to take advantage of us?*

As we sat unmoving, we heard the faint sound of bells. The tinkling noise got louder and louder, until my fifteen-year-old sister suddenly blurted, "It's Santa Claus!" As we all chuckled uncomfortably, someone pounded on the door.

With our eyes riveted on the tiny window in the middle of the door, Dad shuffled forward and cautiously opened the door.

Deborah had been right! Santa Claus *had* found us, despite the narrow back road, despite the cold, dark winter night, and despite—or maybe because of—our desolate circumstances. After Santa handed us candy and fresh fruit, he handed my dad the one thing that could make him find some joy in this holiday season: cold hard cash.

After visiting for a few minutes, Santa departed, leaving behind a family that now believed in miracles. Although Dad patiently explained that our visitor was, in fact, a dear friend from work, simply delivering the money collected by fellow employees, Deborah was never fully convinced. For weeks, she talked about the night Santa visited us. The disdain of others didn't dampen her innocent joy at experiencing the kindness of a fellow human being, whether he was the real thing or not.

And she has continued to believe.

Over the years, Deborah has faced many hardships, including divorce, the death of both parents, and the devastating diagnosis of lung cancer, but through it all, she has managed to maintain a child-like faith in the goodness of mankind. These days, Deborah is the one others turn to in their own desperate times—to borrow her hard-earned money, which may or may not be paid back; to borrow a spare bed for a few nights before they try once again to get life back on track; to borrow a shoulder to cry on. She is always available and willing to help whenever possible.

Now, as I think back on it, I'm convinced Deborah always knew the truth. She knew Santa Claus was real even when others did not. She knew that to some of us, Santa Claus represented a stranger with a big red sack and oodles of candy and presents, but that to others he is a loved one disguised in a red suit and fake beard. And she knew that to others, he is a good-natured coworker bearing much-needed and much-appreciated gifts donated by other coworkers, who care enough to help.

As for me, I knew all along that there was another kind of Santa Claus. This Santa Claus comes disguised as my sister, Deborah, who is always ready with a helping hand or a kind word. But regardless of what disguise Santa Claus takes on when he shows up in our lives, what mattered most yesterday matters most today, and what will still matter most tomorrow is not that Santa Claus's appearance changes depending on the location and the situation, but rather that Santa Claus does in fact exist, as long as we continue to believe.

All that Glitters

BY MARCIA E. BROWN

With the growing interest in all-natural dairy products from cows untreated by hormones, many milk producers are returning to glass bottles with caps, reminiscent of those used in the 1930s and early 1940s. Today's caps feature metallic paper bonded to cardboard color coded to the product within: skim, low fat, or whole milk or cream. In the days before World War II, our favorite dairy, serving eastern Oklahoma, topped its bottles of milk in beautiful foil caps of red, green, gold, and silver aluminum. Whole milk, with its thick layer of cream, buttermilk, skim milk, and whipping cream each had its own identifying color. Twice a week, deliveries to our house made a colorful display.

At the creamery, these bright metal caps were stamped from rolls of thin aluminum. The resulting discarded strips were long "ribbons" of foil about four inches wide, perforated with holes from the punched-out circular caps.

At Christmas, just after the attack on Pearl Harbor, a neighbor who worked for the creamery brought home a bin of these discarded strips, which he thought were pretty. His wife and five children, recycling long before the word was coined (in the 1930s, it was called "making do"), strung the colorful ribbon-like garlands around their Christmas tree, and all the neighbors admired the shiny stuff.

When Mama and I saw our friends' unique decorations, Mama was fascinated. Perhaps it was because that was the Christmas when glittery fragile ornaments, such as shiny balls and icicles, disappeared for what was soon dubbed "the duration of the war," a phrase quickly shortened to The Duration. Even before that fateful month and President Roosevelt's declaration of a state of war, metal had begun to disappear from the domestic scene. Anticipation of the war's needs brought a quick end to the shiny aluminum milk bottle caps, right along with the disappearance of metal coat hangers and wrought iron fences.

On examining our neighbors' idea for using the colorful discards from the dairy, Mama saw that each corner where a circle had been stamped out left a perfect triangle. When our friends offered her a share of their find, Mama started cutting out little triangles from the thin aluminum, sewing them together on her old White pedal sewing machine, and making garlands so lightweight that the slightest movement of air sent them spinning and shimmering.

So was born a cottage industry in our family that flourished for The Duration. At Mama's request, our generous neighbor arrived one day dragging an enormous eight-foot box. Inside was the last of the available milk-cap foil scraps to be found anywhere, as wartime also meant conversion to cardboard caps for milk bottles.

When I hear teachers today trying to explain to children what a million of something looks like, I wish I could show them what a million little aluminum triangles resembled! For surely Mama, Grandma, and I must have cut out a million triangles of foil! We wore out scissors and skin. Mama—never one to let a good idea lie idly—was not only interested in decorating our house, he saw a potential way for us to earn Christmas spending money in the bargain!

For months, during the years of the war, we cut out triangles in the evenings, and by day Mama sewed them into long strips, like tinsel. She also stitched hundreds of short lengths to hang at the ends of Christmas tree branches to replace metallic icicles that had gleamed so invitingly on festive pre-war Christmas trees.

In the fall, we assembled our goods into tissue-paper packets. The prettiest multicolored garlands sold for twenty-five cents; packages of three icicles were ten cents. Around Thanksgiving, we began our sales campaign.

A neighbor's son, also eager to earn spending money, completed our sales force. With Mama following, he and I shopped our wares door to door. We repeated a sales pitch I thought I would never forget, which ended with the declaration that our decorations "will not tarnish, burn nor bust!"

We were a success!

Folks were delighted to buy something new and glittery to decorate with during the drab war years. Young couples just setting up housekeeping were especially glad to buy from us. Each year we sold our entire stock. By December 1944, except for what Mama kept for our own use, we had sold our entire supply.

Even now, sixty-plus years later, I occasionally meet someone who was one of our Christmas decoration customers, or who is the child of a former customer. And true to form— just as we promised—our unusual decorations have not "tarnished, burned, nor busted!"

Each year, as I carefully unpack our WWII Christmas decorations, I think of Mama, Grandma, and I working together to create this lasting holiday glitz made of scraps. And I remember the late autumn evenings, pungent with the smells of the season, when we walked through our small-town neighborhoods to sell our homemade Christmas crafts. And truly there is nothing quite as rewarding as that memory.

The Tea Set

BY MARY L. HARDWICK

It was the most beautiful thing my five-year-old eyes had ever seen—a child-sized porcelain tea set, decorated with redbirds. I was enthralled—in love from that point forward with not only the tea set, but redbirds, too! Best of all, it came in a wooden box that doubled as a miniature storage cabinet. Each perfect little dish had its very own compartment. It was an item I had not even asked for, hadn't even realized I wanted. Thank heavens Santa Claus knew me so well!

I hosted many tea parties for my dolls and stuffed tiger, Jeff, using my little dishes and the child-sized table and chairs my siblings and I shared. Grape juice filled the tiny teapot over and over, which, in turn, was poured into the four dainty teacups. Crackers iced with peanut butter rested on the platter to be shared by all.

Time did not diminish my passion for this most perfect of gifts. My afternoon tea party became an after-school get together. I nibbled on snacks with Jeff and my faithful dolls, as I related all that I had learned in class. Then, one day the unthinkable happened. I rushed home to find my older sister, Terry, using the table as she colored, cut, and glued Valentines. *How dare she!* She knew I always had a tea party after school.

"Terry, you need to leave right now! This is my time," I shouted.

"I'm not moving," Terry replied without looking up. "This table belongs to all of us, and besides Mama told me to work in here." She glanced up at me with a smirk on her face.

That smirk was all it took. Before she had a chance to say another word, I snatched her package of construction paper.

"Give it back!" Terry yelled. She stood up and grabbed at the colored paper, trying to tug it out of my hands. After a few tugs back and forth, I had an idea.

"Here," I said smugly, and abruptly turned loose, intending to make her fall. And fall she did, right up against the dresser behind her—the very dresser my beloved tea set was perched upon.

I watched in horror as the wooden case tipped forward. The individual pieces slid from their compartments, bounced, and then tumbled over the edge, bound for the hard oak floor. The shattering tinkle of breaking glass vibrated in my ears. I stared in shocked dismay at my prized porcelain, now lying in shards.

Not one piece was salvageable.

Heartbroken, I turned to Mama, who promised to replace it. Over the years, I received many different tea sets, though none had redbirds on them. I still have the "replacement" tea sets, but none comes close to meaning as much as that first one did, the one received with a child's delight so many Christmases ago.

Christmas was magical back then. Unexpected gifts, such as the beautiful redbird tea set, were treasures that found a special place in my heart because they were such a wonderful surprise. Don't all adults long to return to childhood, when Christmas was excitement, when the simplest of gifts became cherished memories? Oh, we try to duplicate that joyous time, but because we adults are able to satisfy our wants all year long, surprises become fewer and fewer. Sadly, even our parents, who knew us better than we knew ourselves back then, are no longer able to provide those wonderful "Santa" moments.

Reality and time creep stealthily into our conscience as we age. We lose childhood innocence. When we were children, even the smallest gifts—gifts we hadn't thought to put on our wish list became our most cherished ones. A lowly "Made in China" dime-store tea set, powered only by imagination, cost a pittance in comparison to the electronic items that top most want lists these days; but sometimes, even when the presents are large and expensive, they don't manage to do the trick. Unfortunately, we tend to forget that giving bigger, better, and more-expensive gifts is not what Christmas is all about. We run ourselves ragged trying to find the true spirit of the season, which once again captures that childish anticipation.

Five Christmases ago, Terry presented me with a gift wrapped in red metallic paper, adorned with a golden bow embossed with sprigs of holly. In the maddening way of an adult, which I so hated as a child, I carefully opened the present. I plucked the bow from the top and set it aside, then cautiously lifted each tab of tape, careful not to tear the paper. I even took the time to fold the shiny foil paper and lay it aside for later use.

When I flipped the box over, I was speechless. Tears burned in the back of my throat, and then filled my eyes, blurring the lights on the Christmas tree until they smeared together like a watercolor painting.

"It isn't much," Terry said softly, "but I thought you would like it."

Measured against time and my own adult hands, the miniature redbird tea set I now held in my hands seemed so diminutive, yet each tiny cup overflowed with precious memories. Terry's gift was a link to my past—to our past—and to days of childish abandon. It was tea parties and time spent together, on a little table, on a sick bed, in a blanket tent pitched on dining chairs in the living room, on the back porch, and even on a colorful quilt spread out on the grass under a hot South Carolina sun. The impact on my heart was immeasurable.

Terry passed away recently, and I miss her dearly. Although she assumed her gift wasn't much because it was small, her loving thoughtfulness made it the most cherished gift I have ever received. It will forever represent a lifetime of love and memories between two sisters, and an unspoken apology for an accident that had never been her fault in the first place.

A Doll for Jane

by Barbara Anton

As one of eight children of an impoverished coal miner, Jane had never had a doll. She was aware that her father couldn't afford to buy toys for his six daughters and two sons, but she was confident Santa would bring the doll she yearned for so passionately. She knew that jolly, generous Santa had a workshop at the North Pole where busy elves worked all year long making toys for good little girls and boys.

Each year her heart brimmed with hope, but every Christmas came and went with no doll for Jane. Santa left only a tangerine and a few walnuts in her Christmas stocking.

Each year Jane wished even harder. She remained confident that one day Santa would leave a curly-haired doll that fit perfectly in the crook of her arm. As each Christmas approached, anticipation flowered in her breast. But the years passed, and the doll never materialized.

Eventually, Jane developed into a charming, red-haired beauty. She married, and after two years, a baby boy arrived. She named him Richard David, and she cuddled him, nurtured him, and for Christmas dressed him in short, royal-blue velvet pants and an ivory-hued satin shirt.

As soon as Richard learned to talk, he rebelled. He was the quintessential man's man. There would be no Little Lord Fauntleroy outfits in his closet.

Jane acquiesced, and as each Christmas approached, her meager savings were spent on the little toy trucks, trains, and planes so dear to her little boy's heart. She derived satisfaction from watching him enjoy the rewards of having been a good little boy. Jane was so caught up in his enjoyment, she almost forgot about her longing for a doll under her Christmas tree. Almost.

Jane's generous spirit even extended to me, her niece. One Christmas, she gifted me with the beautiful big doll she had always dreamed of embracing. How she enjoyed watching me cradle that doll in my arms! The doll's hair was arranged to provide a loop for attaching the huge ribbon bows that were worn by children in that era, and she and I changed the doll's hair ribbons frequently, always plumping them to spectacular heights.

In the 1950s, with her son grown and her husband gone, Jane found she had outlived her savings. When looking through the classified pages in search of employment, she came across an ad for assistant to the "doctor" in a doll hospital. She applied immediately. The doctor recognized her love of dolls and her eagerness to assist in their renewal, so even though she had no experience, he hired her.

Working beside the doctor, Jane learned to clean and refurbished dolls to pristine condition before returning them to their owners. She lovingly replaced missing fingers, restuffed damaged bodies, and repaired eyes that no longer closed in sleep.

One day, when the doctor discarded a doll he thought was beyond repair, Jane rescued it from the trash bin. In the comfort of her home, the reconstruction began. Bodywork included replacing one arm, rebuilding several toes, and repairing a chipped tooth.

Jane used a long hatpin to untangle matted hair, one strand at a time. Combed free of tangles, she wound tiny bits of hair on makeshift rollers, and then styled the doll's hair into a mass of golden curls.

Each missing eyelash was individually replaced and crimped. Facial cracks were filled in, cheeks sanded to their original smoothness. With a touch of red, lips once again took on a healthy glow.

When the doll had been restored to perfection, Jane went to Woolworth's Five & Dime on her day off and bought a McCall's doll-clothes pattern. With meticulous care, she cut, basted, and fashioned pale yellow organdy into a dress she then trimmed with white lace. She purchased tiny white shoes and socks and a wide-brimmed straw hat she hand-decorated with daisies and forget-me-nots. Dressed in newly found splendor, Jane's doll resembled a princess. She named the doll Janine, because it sounded like Jane, but was more elegant.

Her masterpiece completed, Jane placed the doll in a box on a bed of white tissue. Wrapping the box in glossy red-and-green paper printed with Christmas trees and wreaths and tying it with a red, tinsel-edged ribbon, Jane set the box on a shelf in her linen closet, where it remained until the night before Christmas.

In the starry silence of Christmas Eve, Jane removed the box from the closet and placed it next to a tiny tree that she had festooned with shiny bells, tinsel, and lights. Then she relaxed in her familiar armchair to watch Lawrence Welk and his carolers on the television. Throughout the evening, she stole furtive glances toward the gaily wrapped package, but refrained from opening it. She retired early, eager for morning to arrive.

On Christmas morning, Jane lay awake in the dusk before dawn, her heart racing with anticipation. As she watched the window for the first hint of sunshine, she felt the years slip away. By the time the golden orb of the sun had crept over the windowsill, Jane was no longer sixty years old, but rather a young six-year-old child, hoping fervently the one gift she had always wanted would be under the tree this year. Jane threw aside the quilt, slipped her feet into slippers, and hurried toward the Christmas tree.

Quivering with delight, she picked up the gaily wrapped box and pulled the end of the silver-edged bow. When the ribbon parted, she slid trembling fingers beneath the red-and-green paper. It crackled and tore away. Then, for the first time in sixty years, Jane, one of eight children born to a poor but hardworking miner, lifted the lid, pushed the tissue paper back, and beheld the exquisite doll that was hers and hers alone.

"Oh, Santa," she whispered, breathlessly. "She's just what I always wanted."

Memories Will Follow

BY CINDY NAPPA MCCABE

I open the door to the cellar and walk down six steps, counting each one as I descend. I want to remember everything—every little thing. I'm alone now, no one to invade my
thoughts. Mom and Dad have departed, off to their new house
across town. Two of my sisters also left, and my other sister
just went outside with her video camera to capture, for the last
time, the outside surroundings of our family home.

I stand at the landing by the door and turn to reach for
the light switch beneath the wall-mounted fixture. I hesitate,
and then decide the grayness of the late afternoon brings in
enough light—just the right amount of light for my melancholy
mood. I start down the next small flight. When I get to the
sixth step, two steps before the end, I stop and look out into
the room. I remember standing here before.

I was eight years old. My cousin, Sharon, stood behind
me, one step above. We sang "Away in the Manger," pretending we were Kathy and Janet Lennon appearing on "Lawrence
Welk's Christmas Special." Despite the fact that everyone in the
crowded room was talking at once, Sharon and I sang on.

Our cousin, Anthony, looked up from his folding chair.
"Shut up, you two! You call that singing?"

We made a face at him and continued singing, louder now. The huge gray and white Formica table was completely covered with platters of fish, tangerines, grapes, cookies, and mixed nuts. The nuts are in their shells, because otherwise they cost too much.

I decided that when I was rich and famous, I would provide unshelled nuts for this party. Salted! *But would Grampa feel badly about not using his special cast-iron nutcracker shaped like a dog?* My sister, Debbie, just five, sat between Grampa and Daddy, trying to crack a nut. Daddy took over and I heard him say, "You can't do this yourself! You have to be careful or you'll crack your fingers!"

"No, I won't!" she yelled.

Daddy gave her one of *those* looks and she quieted down. He held the walnut in place and pushed hard on the dog's tail. The dog's jaws cracked the nut and it spit out shell and nut pieces. Daddy caught them, discarded the shell pieces, then offered the nut pieces to Debbie. She frowned at him, ignoring his offering. So he picked up a piece and ate it himself. She grabbed the rest of it and Grampa laughed. I decided I would also buy shelled nuts.

We stopped singing. No one noticed.

I made my way through the chairs holding aunts, uncles, and cousins until I reached Gramma. She was sitting by the cupboard, close to the large bowl of punch. The bowl looked like crystal, but it was really plastic. Strawberries, once frozen, floated in the red fruit drink.

"Can I have some punch, Gramma?" I asked. Right away, I realized I should have said, "May I?" but Gramma didn't correct me. I know she didn't even mind, because her English was what they call "broken." I liked the way she talked, though, and hoped she never got it fixed.

She looked at me and smiled. I loved her smile. All evening, she had a worried look on her face. It made her look mad, but she wasn't. Mommy says it's because she's nervous that an argument will happen when everyone is together. But I didn't remember there ever being an argument on Christmas Eve. Ever.

Gramma handed me the cup of punch. I pretended the cup was rare crystal and not plastic. I drank my punch quickly, and then asked for another, hoping to get a strawberry this time.

Now, years later, the cellar appears smaller. *However did we all fit?* By the time I was in my teens, older cousins were dating or married, and soon they had children of their own. Before Gramma left this world for a better place, where she would never have to worry about a fight breaking out, she not only had twenty-four grandchildren, but also twenty-four great-grandchildren!

We lived upstairs from Gramma and Grampa. The other families lived nearby, two right next door, and another two just up the street. Until Gramma passed away, we gathered here every Christmas Eve—New Year's Eve, too. It was how we started and ended the holiday season. But that was years ago.

The lowering sun breaks through the clouds and light spills in through the window above the sink, like the lens of a movie camera. Thousands of dust particles dance frantically in its path, and I am transported in time once again.

This time I was twelve years old. Grampa sat at the table sneaking cookies. We laughed at his antics.

"John, no more!" Gramma exclaimed. "Let the others eat!"

Grampa made a face at her when she turned away; we stifled our laughter. Gramma looked crabby again, but she wasn't, really. Except, maybe a little at Grampa.

I watched as Grampa opened the gift Gramma had given him. We all knew what it was. He held up his gift, revealing two white dress shirts.

"Thank you, Clara," he said. "Very nice."

We all agreed, though we'd seen those two shirts before. We raved about how nice they were to stop ourselves from laughing. They were the same two shirts he opened last year, the year before, and even the year before that! Once the festivities were over, Gramma put them back in the drawer at the bottom of his dresser. Next year, she would pull them out and wrap them again.

Lost in my memory, I smile. Gramma was passing out Christmas envelopes. When she handed me mine, I thanked her and opened it quickly, even though I knew what I would find. I took out three crisp, brand-new one-dollar bills. They were so perfect—no creases or marks at all. I thought they must have been made for her to give us. Even though the older grandchildren knew you couldn't buy much with three dollars, we all appreciated it.

Sweet, dear Gramma. She was like the woman in the bible who had so little, but gave it all. *That is true giving,* I think, as my eyes roam lovingly around the tables, over the precious faces. That's what Christmas always was in this house, what Christmas always should be.

I hear my sister Kathi call my name, and the Christmas party disappears.

"Cindy?" she calls. "Are you down here?"

I walk to the bottom of the stairs and look up to see her standing on the landing. "Yep," I reply. "Just taking one last look."

"I know," she says, walking down a few steps.

One glance at her red swollen eyes and I know she's been crying. She understands that this place was where the best Christmases took place. She understands, and is having as much trouble as I am walking away and leaving our memories behind.

Finally, we can stay no longer. "Let's go," I say.

We walk back up the stairs, our legs heavy with regret. Without turning around, we exit. But when next our hearts seek Christmas and our thoughts return in time to this house, this basement, we discover the truth—all the memories born here have clung to our souls and moved with us.

Love for Father

BY LESE DUNTON

We lived in New Jersey—surrounded by trees—in what my father referred to as "a curious old house." On Christmas Eve, we had a family tradition. Actually, we had several, but my favorite one was when my father read *'Twas the Night Before Christmas* to the family.

It wasn't so much the way he read the story, placing the same comforting emphasis on the same reliable sentences each year. Nor was it the way we three children snuggled up in our pajamas, smiling and excited. These elements were important, but it had more to do with the fact that my father was sober.

I didn't know why I loved him so much that night every year. I didn't realize it was because, for some reason, he decided not to drink. I just knew he was present among the presents. He was really there: warm, caring, enchanting.

He would read aloud with great theatrical flair, "And what to my wondering eyes should appear, but a miniature sleigh and eight tiny reindeer." I didn't want it to end. I knew in the morning he'd be distant again, disappearing to "check the garage" or get something out of the basement. Soon, he would act strange and not pay any attention to me. The next thing I knew, he'd be asleep in front of the television and my mother would be sad.

Another tradition was to make sandwiches for Santa Claus. Surely, he would appreciate the nourishment after such a long trip. My two older brothers knew that Santa was actually Dad, but I had not yet discovered this fact. You can imagine my horror when one Christmas Eve they told me of their prank: pouring Tabasco sauce on Santa's snacks. I assumed the red-suited man, nice as he was, would be upset and hurt. Who could blame him? A naughty act had been committed—which I was unable to prevent—and Christmas would certainly be canceled!

Miraculously, the next morning everything proceeded beautifully. I learned, years later, that Dad thought it had been very funny. He had a great sense of humor; he never got upset about anything—even when there was a need for concern. "No problem" was one of his favorite sayings.

One year, when I was a teenager, he gave me a big, hard-cover book called *The Synonym Finder,* and on it he wrote, To MY FAVORITE DAUGHTER, WHO LOVES WORDS AND THINGS; WHO IS XMAS. I was his favorite daughter because I was his only daughter. Our cornball humor connection was strong.

I often search for synonyms in the book he gave me—just for the fun of it—and when I read his inscription to me again, I remember the holidays and how much love and vitality were within him. He wouldn't always speak the words in depth or at length, but he could write them, and he could communicate with his sparkling blue eyes.

"We have to have a Yule Log for Christmas!" he'd proclaim excitedly, with the wide-eyed wonder of a kid, as the big day approached. This announcement was followed by stomping around outside to locate the biggest piece of wood on the property.

"How about this one, Dad?" I would finally ask.

"No," he'd whisper, "I have a special one all picked out."

Eager to see the log he'd already picked out, I walked behind him, into the woods where the perfect log was finally revealed. This outing was even more adventurous when punctuated by a snowstorm, which we both loved profoundly. In later years, whenever it snowed, we called each other on the phone and said the same things: "Have you looked outside?" and "Think snow!"

His enthusiasm for snow and life never faltered. Still, I wished for longer talks.

On winter nights, an enormous fireplace lit up our living room with warmth and light and crackling wood. We sat quietly, mesmerized by the powerful flames. On one holiday, we began talking about a friend of ours who hadn't had a drink in a very long time. Dad looked deeply into my eyes and said, "I admire him. I just can't . . ." Instead of finishing his sentence, his eyes continued to talk to me. I replied—without words and holding his gaze—that it was okay. I understood and loved him very much. At that moment, my mother walked in announcing dinner, and the subject was never broached again.

A few years later, he was diagnosed with liver cancer. Fortunately, he was able to stay at home with his family at his side. His bed was moved next to a big window, where he could see the snow falling softly against the bare trees.

He had always predicted he would die quickly, "Like a one-horse open shay!" When I asked what he meant by that, he explained that for years the horse was strong and pulling the weight of the cart, and then one day it would just drop dead unexpectedly. True to his word, he was chopping wood and painting the house with great vigor right up until his illness struck. Once it hit, he made his transition within a couple of weeks; no long, drawn-out illness for him.

I see him clearly now, sitting on the couch with the classic Christmas book in his lap and his three children gathered around him. I can't help but smile at the perfect picture we make, and my heart is healed when I remember those Christmases we always enjoyed. The pop and crack from the fire is a caress to my ears. The fireplace heat radiates into the cozy living room, the colorful tree lights twinkle gently, and familiar holiday music in the background lets me know that all is well. I see Dad tip his head to one side—as if listening—then, pointing his finger up to the sky he announces in his most awe-filled voice, "And so, he exclaimed, as he rode out of sight, Merry Christmas to all and to all a good night!"

Contributors

MICHAEL M. ALVAREZ ("Holiday Visitors"), a native of Arizona, has been writing for over thirty years. His stories, poems, and articles have appeared in the *Arizona Daily Star*, *Writer's Digest*, and several anthologies. His novels include *The Last Place God Made*, *Deliver Us From Evil*, and *The Treasure of the Santa Ritas*.

BESS ANTISDALE ("A Gift of Love") enjoys baking bread and cookies for her real dollies: five children, thirteen grandchildren, and seven great-grandchildren. Bess is a seminar conference speaker, author, and twenty-seven year radio-broadcast newsletter columnist. Her work also appears in several magazines, including *Moody Monthly* and *Campus Life*. Her husband, Wilbur J. Antisdale, is Pastor Emeritus at Westminster Chapel in Bellevue, WA.

BARBARA ANTON ("A Doll for Jane"), of Sarasota, Florida, has received over two hundred awards for writing. Two books, *Terse Verse* and *Savories*, are available online. Look for her upcoming work, *Egrets to the Flames*, *50 Award-Winning Feature Articles*, and *Demi Verse*, due out soon. Barbara, who is listed in *Who's Who in America*, passed away before this book was finalized.

RAYMOND L. ATKINS ("The Christmas Gifts") resides in Rome, Georgia. His work has been published in *Christmas Stories from Georgia*, *The Lavender Mountain Anthology*, and *The Blood and Fire Review*. His first novel, *The Front Porch Prophet*, will be published in 2008. Currently, Raymond is at work on *Sorrow Wood*, his second novel.

DMITRI BARVINOK ("The Last Apple") is a high-school sophomore, living in Ann Arbor, Michigan. Among his many goals, he hopes to one day author his own book.

DOROTHY BAUGHMAN ("A Special Christmas Card"), a freelance writer for over thirty years, has had numerous stories, along with children's and adult's books (including ebooks), published. Dorothy lives in her hometown and writes a weekly column for the local newspaper. She and her husband of forty-seven years have three children and seven grandchildren.

DELBERT L. BIEBER ("Safely Home" and "The Empty Chair") is pastor of First Church of the Nazarene in Toms River, New Jersey, where he has been a pastor for thirteen years; all total, Delbert has been pastoring for thirty-two years. Delbert, married to Patsy, is the father of two sons and grandfather to a one-year-old girl.

ARTHUR BOWLER ("At the Five and Dime"), a U.S./Swiss citizen and graduate of Harvard Divinity School, is a writer and speaker in English and German. His work has appeared in several bestselling anthologies and in bestselling books in Switzerland. Look for his book *A Prayer and a Swear* or visit *www.arthurbowler.ch*.

MARCIA E. BROWN ("All that Glitters" and "Wishing for Miracles") began writing her family stories fifteen years ago to preserve them for her son. Since then, much of her work has appeared in magazines and anthologies. Marcia hopes to publish a book of her own work soon. The birth of a grandson gave new impetus to her writing goals, as she now also writes for children.

LINDA BRUNO ("Yes, Deborah, There Really is a Santa Claus") is a writer, speaker, and trainer. She is writing a devotional book based on how our interactions with pets mirror our relationship with God. Linda and husband, Guy, have one grown daughter, five grandchildren, and three "fur" kids. Linda can be reached at *lfbruno@cfl.rr.com.*

RANDY JEAN BRUSKRUD ("Disappearing Act"), using her pen name, Randy Jeanne, has published one romantic suspense novel and has sold work to *True Romance Magazine.*

RENIE BURGHARDT ("Memories of a Refugee Camp Christmas") is a freelance writer who was born in Hungary. She came to the United States in 1951, and has since been published in over fifty anthologies and many magazines. E-mail her at: *renie_burghardt@yahoo.com.*

CARRILLEE COLLINS BURKE ("Miracles") has been published in many magazines, and is the winner of numerous writing contests. She is the author of one romance/mystery novel. In 2001, she was nominated for the Pushcart Prize by Dana Literary Society. Carrillee resides in Florida with her novelist husband, Ned Burke.

CONNIE STURM CAMERON ("The School Desks") has been married to Chuck for twenty-eight years. Together, they have two children, Chase and Chelsea, and a daughter-in-law, Elizabeth. Connie is the author of *God's Gentle Nudges,* and she has also been featured in dozens of periodicals and anthologies. Contact her at: *www.conniecameron.com* or *conniec@ netpluscom.com.*

J. Hogan Clark ("Shared Popcorn"), a former employee of the Office of Naval Intelligence, is active in community affairs in Sedalia, Missouri, where he currently lives. In addition, Jack is a freelance writer and songwriter and enjoys spending his free moments on the front porch strumming on an acoustic guitar.

Helen C. Colella ("Getting it Right") is a freelance writer from Colorado. Her work includes educational materials (geography and history workbooks), articles, and stories for adults and children. Helen is contributor to nine anthologies and numerous parenting magazines, and currently operates her own business, AssistWrite, where she offers writing and consultation services to independent publishers.

Christine E. Collier ("Christmas Eve Delivery") has been published in many children's magazines and is the author of six books: *The Writer's Club*; *Mystery is Our Shadow*; *Christmas at Cliffhanger Inn*; *Something Borrowed, Something Blue*; *Adventure on Apple Orchard Road*; and *Twelve Months of Mystery*. Her most recent book is titled *A Holiday Sampler*.

Charlene A. Derby ("A Christmas Aha!") is a freelance writer who lives in Southern California with her husband and son. It is her belief that blogging is the best way to keep in touch with the "fearsome foursome" and their extended families. Her previously published stories have appeared in several compilation books and in the magazines *Reminisce Extra* and *Focus on the Family*.

LESE DUNTON ("Love for Father") is the founder and editor of the online publication The New Sun *(www.newsun.com).* Lese has worked for *Village Voice Newspaper, New York Daily News,* CBS Television, *Life* magazine, and *Wall Street Journal* in a variety of positions, including editor, producer, writer, and designer.

SHAUNA SMITH DUTY ("Getting Christmas") is a freelance copywriter and full-time copy director. Her world revolves around language. She believes that words magically transfer ideas from one mind to another and have the power to make people laugh. Shauna practices the literary arts to spread peace, love, and happiness throughout the world.

NANCY JO ECKERSON ("Growing Up Cool") is a freelance writer and Ethical Wills facilitator from Akron, NY. Eckerson, a contributing writer for the *Buffalo News, Forever Young Magazine,* and numerous other publications, is an editor, and copywrites for corporate endeavors and Web sites as well. She's older and wiser now, but still cool!

MARIE (NIKKI) ESSELSTEIN ("All I Want for Christmas") is a graduate of the Ohio State University (English and history). Currently, she works in administration for the American Motorcyclist Association. Marie feels like the luckiest person in the world to have a happy, healthy extended family that includes her teenage son, her parents, and both grandmothers.

BARBARA JEANNE FISHER ("Sometimes Less is More" and "Through the Innocence of Childhood") writes using the words of her heart to touch the hearts of others. The author of several children's books and editor of *The Voices of Alcohol* and *The Voices of Lung Cancer,* Barbara is pleased to show her work in various anthologies and magazines. She teaches online writing for Writer's College, and lives in Ohio with her husband and seventeen grandchildren. Look for the sequel to her novel *Stolen Moments* soon.

JO E. GRAY ("Santa is Real") was born the fourth in a family of five children. Her early years were spent on a farm in North Central Texas, where she attended classes in a one-room schoolhouse. She graduated from Midwestern University in Wichita Falls, married, and became the mother of two girls. A retired schoolteacher, Jo currently lives in Arizona with her husband of fifty years and their twelve-year-old dog.

NELIA J. GREER ("Grandpa Will's Gift") has lived in Arizona since 1970, and was married to Ralph for fifty-four years. Their marriage produced four children and ten grandchildren. Nelia is a devoted writer for her church, and has been published in a number of periodicals. Her favorite topic is family history. She is a longtime member of The Fountain Hills Christian Writers Group.

SHIRLEY P. GUMERT ("The Stranger with the Cardboard Suitcase") is a freelance writer who lives in West Kerr County, Texas. She has had her work published in the *Santa Fe (New Mexico) Reporter,* several other New Mexico newspapers, the *Houston Chronicle's* Texas Magazine, *The Rocking Chair Reader: Coming home,* and *Classic Christmas: True Stories of Holiday Cheer and Goodwill.*

Mary L. Hardwick ("The Tea Set"), who spent her childhood traveling the world as a military brat, found her calling in South Carolina, where she is employed as a day care director. Mary received a degree in Early Childhood Education in 1985 at USC. In addition to writing in various genres, she enjoys reading Western fiction.

M. DeLoris Henscheid ("My Long Brown Stockings"), along with her husband Bernard, has nine children and thirty-one grandchildren. DeLoris graduated from Idaho State University at the age of fifty-four with a degree in Early Childhood Education. Since retirement, she has enjoyed writing about family, and has had a number of stories published in Adams Media Anthologies and in *Idaho Magazine.*

Ann Hite ("The Christmas Tree Hunter") has had her work appear in numerous publications, including *The Dead Mule, Fiction Warehouse, The SiNK, A Cup of Comfort®,* several additional anthologies, *Moonwort Review, Plum Biscuit,* and *Poor Mojo's Almanac.* Ann has a large family, over 1,000 books, a flower garden, and her laptop. Feel free to visit her Web site, The Painted Door, at *http://home.bellsouth .net/p/pwp-painteddoor.*

Georgia A. Hubley ("Mother Nature to the Rescue") and her husband live in Henderson, Nevada. She has two grown sons. Her work has appeared in various anthologies and magazines, including *Plus Magazine, Christian Science Monitor, Birds and Bloom Magazine, Story Circle Journal, Capper's, Good Old Days Magazine,* and *Senior Wire Syndicate,* as well as other national magazines and newspapers. Contact her at *GEOHUB@aol.com.*

MARILYN JASKULKE ("The Lonely Christmas Tree") is a published writer; her work appears in several inspirational anthologies and Christian publications. Originally from Minnesota, Marilyn resides with her husband in Mission Viejo, California. She is the mother of four sons, eleven grandchildren, and the great-grandmother of three. Her hobbies include playing bridge, golfing, and sewing quilts for the mission field.

JEWELL JOHNSON ("A Million Stars Looked Down") writes from Arizona, where she lives with her husband, LeRoy. Together, they have six children and eight grandchildren. Jewell, a retired registered nurse, currently works as a part-time caregiver and leads a writing group. She keeps involved with children by babysitting her three young grandsons and teaching children in her church. When relaxing, Jewell reads, quilts, and takes walks.

BARBARA KIFFIN ("Burnt Toast and Tinsel") is retired after twenty-three years as Public Relations Manager for the Eastern Monmouth Area Chamber of Commerce in Red Bank, New Jersey. She was also editor and lead writer for the Chamber's newsletter, *The Leading Edge*. Barbara has three glorious offspring and three magnificent granddaughters. She lives alone and is as happy as a clam.

MIMI GREENWOOD KNIGHT ("In the Nick of Time") is a freelance writer living in South Louisiana with her husband, David, four kids, four dogs, four cats, and one knuckle-headed bird. Her work has appeared in *Parents, American Baby, Working Mother, Campus Life, Christian Parenting Today, In Touch, At-Home Mother,* and *Today's Christian Woman* magazines, and assorted Web sites and anthologies.

EMMARIE LEHNICK ("Let There be Light"), of Amarillo, Texas, is a retired teacher with a B.S. and M.A. in English/Speech. She is a member of Inspirational Writers Alive, and has been published in magazines as well as in *Christian Miracles, The Rocking Chair Reader,* and three volumes of *A Cup of Comfort*®. She and her husband have one daughter, one son, and four grandsons.

HELEN LUECKE ("The Perfect Gift") lives in Amarillo, Texas, with her husband Richard. Helen is cofounder of Inspirational Writers Alive! Amarillo Chapter. She writes short stories, articles, and devotionals, and has been published in several anthologies, as well as other inspirational publications.

VIVIENNE MACKIE ("Time of Delight") left her small Rhodesia village and ended up in South Africa, then the United States, to pursue careers in psychology and ESL. Her sisters still live in Zimbabwe and South Africa, but even though separated by many miles, they continue to be very close.

CINDY NAPPA MCCABE ("Memories Will Follow") has wanted to be a writer since she was seven years old. Fifty-one years later, Cindy has begun to seriously follow her childhood dream. She lives with her loving husband, Rodney, and her seventeen-year-old cat, Pachelbel Canon, and is grateful for close family and friends. Currently, Cindy enjoys writing stories that revolve around the memories of her extended family, whom helped make her childhood wonderful.

LYNN RUTH MILLER ("An Aunt Sunne Christmas" and "Santa's Messenger") had stories—"Thoughts While Walking the Dog" and "More Thoughts While Walking the Dog"—published in 2001. Lynn Ruth has also published two novels: *Starving Hearts* (May 2000) and *The Late Bloomer* (2005). Her storytelling shows are presented regularly in San Francisco and at the Edinburgh Festival Fringe in Scotland.

BRIDGET BALTHROP MORTON ("The Truth about Santa") freely admits her favorite feast during the holidays is St. Stephen's Day. She adores sitting by the fire, glass of brandy in hand, with nothing to do but admire her tree and the crumpled wrapping paper at her feet.

KATHLEEN M. MULDOON ("The Baby Jesus Bed") teaches writing for the Institute of Children's Literature. She has authored sixteen books and numerous magazine articles and stories for children. When not writing, she enjoys playing with her cat, Prissy, and her parakeet, Abraham, at her home in San Antonio, Texas.

AMY AMMONS MULLIS ("A Different Kind of Carol") lives in upstate South Carolina with a black Lab and a spoiled Dachshund, instead of a reindeer team. She works as a church secretary, but if she ever grows up, she hopes to live the adventurous life of an elf. Read more of her essays in *Letters to My Mother: Tributes to the Women Who Give Us Life—and Love* and *A Cup of Comfort® for Writers* (2007).

CLAUDIA MCKINNEY MUNDELL ("Giving and Receiving") grew up in Kansas, but writes from Carthage, Missouri, where she lives with her husband. The mother of two grown sons, Claudia has taught Language Arts in Missouri schools, been active in library work, dabbled at weaving, loves to visit historic places, and enjoys music from the '40s through the '60s.

MATTHIAS L. NISKA ("An Inexpensive Gift") holds degrees in Music Education and History from Concordia College in Moorhead, Minnesota. His writing interests include character-driven, Christian-oriented fiction, poetry, and personal experience pieces. His poem, "A Writer's Prayer," will appear in an upcoming issue of *The Christian Communicator*. He resides in Andover, Minnesota.

MARILYN OLSEIN ("Dancing with Daddy") retired from her career in Detroit's automotive industry and is now a freelance writer living in Mobile, Alabama. She is a charter member of the Mobile Writers' Guild and is in the process of completing her second novel.

LINDA KAULLEN PERKINS ("Christmas Giving") has had her work appear in *Bylines 2007 Writer's Desk Calendar, The Rocking Chair Reader* series, *A Cup of Comfort® for Weddings,* and *Classic Christmas* by Adams Media. She is a member of Romance Writers of America, the Missouri Writers' Guild, and a critique group. For more information, check out her Web site: *http://hometown.aol.com/squatters5/lindakaullenperkins .html.*

CHERYL K. PIERSON ("The Adventures of Baby Jesus") lives in Oklahoma City with her husband and two "almost-grown" children. Currently, she is working on her sixth novel and a screenplay adaptation. Cheryl teaches writing workshops in the Oklahoma City metro area.

CONNIE VIGIL PLATT ("Window Shopping") has finally realized her lifelong dream of becoming a published author. A number of her short stories have been published both online and in print. Her novel, *Pair A Dice,* can be found at all major bookstores.

CAROLINE B. POSER ("Boy to the World!"), the mother of three sons, is a technology marketing manager by day and moonlights as an author and columnist. For more information visit her Web site at: *www.CarolinePoser.com.*

DEBRA J. RANKIN ("Finding Santa") enjoys reading mysteries and nonfiction. When not baking cookies, knitting, or working in her garden, Debra is working on a memoir about her father.

FRANCES HILL ROBERTS ("A Good Song for Shaving") is a retired family therapist who recently returned to school to follow her dream of writing. Frances, a grandmother with a passion for the written word, hopes readers enjoy her account of her happiest and most innocent Christmas.

Bob Rose ("The Hairbrush") is a husband, father, and grandfather. He enjoys cooking and rehabbing his eighty-year-old house. Bob has been a carpenter, music teacher, pastor, counselor, and salesman. He has written for numerous magazines, devotionals, and book anthologies. He makes his home in Wyoming.

Joan Fitting Scott ("So Little, So Much") is an award-winning freelance writer. She is the author of *Skinning the Cat: A Baby Boomer's Guide to the New Retiree Lifestyles*. She has written for *www.office.com* and *www.goworldtravel.com,* and her work has appeared in *Distinctive Lifestyles*, *Where*, *Key*, *The Fort Worth Business Press*, *The Fort Worth Star-Telegram*, and *Greensboro News and Record,* as well as several anthologies. She is a member of the Freelance Writers Network and lives in Fort Worth, Texas.

Al Serradell ("A Musical Miracle"), a Los Angeles native, is a veteran writing instructor in the Oklahoma City area. A professional journalist, Al has worked for newspapers in Oklahoma (*Journal Record* and *Guthrie News Leader*) and Colorado (*Rocky Mountain News*), and co-owns an editorial business, FabKat Editorial Services, *www.westwindsmedia.com*.

Sharon Sheppard ("Mother Knows Best") is a wife, mother, grandmother to five boys, and freelance writer, living in Central Minnesota. A former college English instructor, she has also taught English as a Second Language in Riga, Latvia. Her fiction and nonfiction pieces have appeared in scores of magazines and anthologies.

FAITH SHERRILL ("Belonging to Winter") was born in Phoenix, Arizona, in 1983. Twenty-two years later, she moved to California, where she has worked a number of jobs while writing her first novel, *Moon Child*.

LYNNE COOPER SITTON ("Some Gifts Cannot Be Wrapped") has published stories, verses, and illustrations in anthologies, greeting cards, and on the children's Web site for Focus for Family. Lynne and her husband live in South Florida, where she is president of the American Christian Writers' Association. Besides her sons, Lynne also has two granddaughters who will hear their great-great-grandmother's stories.

RITA H. STRONG ("The Sweeping Angel") resides with her husband of sixty years in Holyoke, Massachusetts. Her articles and stories have appeared in national and local publications. Rita directs a "Fun in Writing" class at the Senior Center in the city.

DONNA SUNDBLAD ("Forty Dollars") is a freelance writer and author. She lives in rural Georgia with her husband and flock of pets. Donna shares the joy of storytelling with her grandchildren, and her love of writing spreads beyond the pages of her books to workshops, the development and teaching of online writers' classes, and a monthly column for writers. Her books *Pumping Your Muse* and *Windwalker* are available in print or ebook format. For more information, visit Donna's Web site at *www.theinkslinger.net*.

ANNEMARIEKE TAZELAAR ("The Saint and the Santa"), born in the Netherlands, moved to Michigan after World War II. She has lived her adult life in Washington State as a teacher and business owner, and spends her spare time writing. One of her stories is featured in *The Rocking Chair Reader,* and several articles appear in the *A Cup of Comfort®* collection.

CHERIE TROPED ("A Gift for Veronica") is the author of three children's books. An award-winning journalist and playwright, Cherie is a contributing writer for *The Los Angeles Times* and other national and regional publications. A graduate of St. Joseph's College with a Bachelor of Arts degree in English, she lives and writes in Los Angeles.

PATSY THOMAS ("Seeing is Believing") is currently working on her first full-length project, a historical time-travel romance novel. She loves to travel and read, and has worked in the banking industry for the past twenty-five years. Patsy has two grown sons, and lives with her husband, Joseph, and pug dog, Picabo, in Yukon, Oklahoma.

WAYNE R. WALLACE ("Home for the Holidays"), now retired from the local electric utility company in Oklahoma City, is a college professor working on his first novel. His story "A Bike for Christmas" was published in *Classic Christmas: True Stories of Holiday Cheer and Goodwill.*

STELLA WARD WHITLOCK ("Grandpa's Love") is the wife of a Presbyterian minister, mother of four, grandmother of seven, writer, and teacher. Stella currently teaches at Methodist University, Fayetteville, North Carolina.

MEGAN (MOLLY) D. WILLOME ("The Sweetness of Giving") contributes to *Wacoan,* a monthly lifestyle magazine, volunteers her time and expertise on newsletters for nonprofit organizations, and also writes for *Directions: The Magazine of the Texas Hill Country.* Additionally, Megan's work has been included in several anthologies.

LESLIE J. WYATT ("Evergreen") is a freelance writer for children and adults, with more than eighty articles and stories accepted for publication, as well as a middle-grade historical novel, *Poor is Just a Starting Place* (Holiday House). Leslie and her husband of twenty-four years have six children and live in an 1880s farmhouse in rural Missouri.

About the Editor

Helen Szymanski and her high school sweetheart, Thomas Polaski, have been married for thirty-two years and have three grown children of whom they are very proud.

Over the course of her career, Helen has progressed from poet to essayist, photojournalist to author, and newspaper editor to book editor. As an enjoyable pastime, Helen keeps the magic of her own childhood Christmases alive through her Web site *www.theelfdoor.com,* where she designs elf doors, a hobby she began when she was eight years old. Contact her at *hkpolaski@yahoo.com.*